Dear Kelly,

Life is Always Happe
For us All!! ♡

With Big Love,

Me

Me

Life Guide and Guided J*urney by Journal
Featuring 11 Weeks of 7 Soul:Minds Exercises

Jennifer Ayers-Belinkis

© 2018 by Jennifer Ayers-Belinkis
First Printing, 2018
ISBN: 173201860X
ISBN-13: 9781732018600
Library of Congress Control Number: 2018902134
HOPE International Publishing, Richmond, VA

Cover design by Ronny Piotraut

 Printed in the United States of America on Recycled Paper

My deepest gratitude radiates out to the
people, places, things, and events of my life
that have supported and influenced me in becoming
who I am today, I appreciate and thank you all.

And a special thanks to you.
With your purchase of
Me: Life Guide and Guided Journey by Journal,
you are supporting
HOPE—Home t**O P**urpos**E,**
a nonprofit organization
dedicated to
inspiring,
motivating,
empowering,
and supporting
YOU to create
greater personal, community, and environmental
awareness and development.

Thank **YOU**
for your support.
It matters.
YOU MATTER!

Contents

Who looks outside, dreams; who looks inside, awakes.
—CARL JUNG (1875—1961)

Introduction

One of life's greatest ironies is that we will always want what we think we don't have; but if we look close enough we will always have exactly what we need.

ME: LIFE GUIDE and Guided Journey by Journal was written using a compilation of life-transforming questions that I have asked myself for years but only recently have I endeavored to search within *me* to discover the answers. Every question can be answered, self-communication and self-awareness are the keys to receiving the answers that are suitable for you while taking into consideration that every human being is unique and different.

This guide is constructed of two parts:
Part 1 – The *Life Guide* explains in simple diagrams and terminology the basics of human nature, life experiences, who we are, and how human beings function. Although I have used my own life experiences as the greatest source and reference for the material in this guide, I have also included many additional references. Scientific research studies, as well as other documented facts, are mentioned to reinforce and further your knowledge and understanding of each subject. Repetition is used throughout this guide on purpose. Repeating many of the concepts and facts that are explained here will spark your consciousness and instill them in your conscious, subconscious and unconscious **Minds**, that is of course if you choose to instill them.

My goal in writing this guide was to compile and simplify complex and pertinent information of which I believe every human being should become aware of at some point in their life. What you do with what you read and learn here is your choice. One of the greatest discoveries and realizations that I have made throughout this process is the way in which I have been living my life has always been **my** choice.

It's your life, it's your reality, and it's your choice.
Life happens but you most definitely
choose how you live your life.

Part 2 – The *Guided Journey by Journal* is a collection of **7 Soul:Minds Exercises** that when answered consecutively for 11 weeks can instill and reinforce habits of self-communication leading to greater self-awareness, unconditional love, gratitude, as well as setting and accomplishing goals, to name a few. Almost every book I have read, lectures that I have attended, and information that I have gathered pertaining to personal development and transformation emphasizes the importance of the 7 subjects that make up the **7 Soul:Minds Exercises** located here in this guide. I have discovered that reading and attending lectures, and so on, are all wonderful ways to advance personal development but real, lasting, life transformations happen when you *do* something with what you have learned and by answering the **7 Soul:Minds Exercises** you are *doing*.

The questions that are asked in the journal part of this guide are precise and by answering them consecutively they are able to support and build new neurological pathways to your brain, consequently creating the life you choose. That is, of course, if you choose to self-communicate in order to create more unconditional love, happiness, and gratitude in your life in addition to making your goals, hopes and dreams become your reality.

I have learned to enjoy *my* life and to always *question* it in order to discover the answers that can only come from within me and I have come to believe we were born to do just that!

PART 1

Life Guide

CHAPTER 1

Origins

Knowing yourself is the beginning of all wisdom.
—ARISTOTLE (384—322 BC)

My "Old" Story

HAVE YOU EVER FELT AND/OR THOUGHT THAT MAYBE LIFE IS PASSING YOU BY?

FOR YEARS, I felt stuck in life, blocked. An emptiness existed within me, and as much as I tried, I couldn't seem to fill it. It felt as if I was going nowhere, even though I thought I'd been almost everywhere. Living a life of routine, in which each day ended with about the same outcome as the day that came before it, I felt unfulfilled. Day after day and night after night, I was cut off from really living and had succumbed to merely existing, as if I were a robot running on an automated system and just going through the motions.

I surrendered my time, my attention, and pretty much all I had to give to others—family members, friends, and strangers. Please allow me to make myself clear: Giving your time and energy to others is a wonderful thing, but when you are giving to everyone except yourself, at some point in your life, you will feel the impact. When your inner self is not stable, secure, and balanced—in harmony—it is only a matter of time before you become aware of it somehow. My personal experience taught me that mental and physical pains are the repercussions of self-neglect/self-punishment.

It never occurred to me to treat myself as I treated others, to care enough about myself to self-communicate, and to love myself unconditionally in every moment, exactly how I am in the moment. I mostly judged and criticized myself. At the time, I was the last person I wanted to communicate with; I was downright depressing.

From a bystander's perspective, my life must have seemed like a fairy tale. My friends and family had no idea that I was going through a life crisis—depression—and the greatest paradox was that I didn't even know it myself at the time. I knew something wasn't quite right, but as I looked around me, it seemed everyone had their problems and lived their lives in quite the same manner as I did—just getting through the day only to relive it all over again the next day.

I am very grateful to be the wife of an amazing, supportive man, and together we raise our four inspiring children and one frisky dog. But for years, I would wake up each morning after eight hours (or more) of sleep, drained of energy; thinking that the best years of my life were over; feeling old and worn-out and blaming myself, my childhood, and others for the results of my life.

Many thoughts echoed through my head: thoughts of how I had wasted my life, thoughts that seemingly screamed out the fact that I wasn't good enough or worthy enough. *Why me?* I wondered. *What is wrong with me?* The influences of these thoughts and feelings prompted my actions and behavior. I had absolutely no motivation or inspiration to get out of bed and start the day. *For what?* I loved my family and friends, and they were the only reason I eventually got out of bed—to do for others. Deep down, I knew that this was not really living. I struggled each day with feelings of being constrained and frustrated.

Back then, life seemed more like a chore than a gift. Self-sabotage, day after day, became a habit of mine. I had unconsciously decided to self-destruct, and my weapons of choice were consuming unhealthy foods and indulging in bouts of anger, frustration, and worry, to name a few. Something wasn't right, and for years I sought help from professionals (teachers, medical and holistic practitioners, therapists, and so on) in various fields, hoping to receive answers to my questions:

What is true happiness?
What is true love?
Why do I feel, act/behave, and think in this way?
Is this *all* that life has to offer?
Why do I feel drained of energy and tired most of the day?
I have all that I ever dreamed of. I volunteer and give of myself for the good of others. What is missing?

The responses I received varied over the years, but one specific piece of advice stuck with me. Many of these professionals replied that the answers come from within the questioner. At the time, this was *most definitely not* the answer that I wanted to hear; it didn't make sense. For many years, I couldn't comprehend what they meant. These professionals left me even more confused, and when I thought of the time and money I had spent only to receive roughly the same answer, I became frustrated and even infuriated. I was exhausted, and at times, so was my bank account. With absolutely no strength, energy, or any clue how to discover the answers that were supposedly hidden within me I desperately kept searching for outside support, someone—anyone—who would know what to do and how to do it. I wanted to feel alive and worthy of living my life.

Years of therapy with no apparent answer led me to study alternative therapies and other subjects for myself, hoping to discover the answers that would come from within me. Study and practice finally brought me to the realization that my biggest obstacle back then was the fear of what

I might discover hiding deep within me. I truly believed that my time and energy was only sufficient to take care of mandatory tasks, and it was to be used for family, work, and studies. I feared that if I were to search within, I would definitely lose control, fall apart, collapse, and be unable to function. I was barely holding on to what I had. Taking care of me was just another chore—more work and one more thing to add to the to-do list. What would I find out? Could I handle it? What would happen with my family? And if that wasn't enough reason to avoid investigating myself, where would I find the time? I didn't know how to self-investigate or search within anyway, and I convinced myself that all was well—that's life; just carry on.

I carried on, all right. I carried on with the same **E**motions, **A**ctions/behaviors, and **T**houghts (I will refer to them as **EAT**s) for years, forcing a smile and hiding my true feelings and thoughts from everyone—worst of all, from myself. I realize now that I had created life habits of blame, guilt, feeling sorry for myself, and telling myself again and again that I was not worthy. I truly believed that I wasn't courageous and/or strong enough to handle the truth of my life and come face to face with the person I had become. My perspective of who I had become consisted of a weak, lazy, scared coward with no right to enjoy life. I thought that facing the truth, gaining more knowledge of who I had become would only magnify more of my negative qualities, damper my perspective on life, and destroy the little spirit, positivity, that I had left and was so desperately holding on to. Back then, I believed that my life was a hopeless cause as I searched for someone or thing to save me. The only way I could turn my life around was to face these very same **EAT**s that had gotten me where I was and had dominated me. But how?

Me: Life Guide and Guided Journey by Journal is a tool that I created and developed to support me in coming face to face with myself. My own search for the answers to the question, "Who am I, really?" have brought me to the conclusion that the answers to any question you could ever ask yourself truly do come from within the individual. With patience and practice, I developed positive self-communication skills that shed more light on who I had become in order to reveal my true authentic self.

Truly live while you are alive!

Life's Creations

Today, I can honestly say that life is extraordinary. I love the fact that I can wake up each morning with great anticipation for the day ahead. I go to sleep each night with gratitude and with an overall feeling of contentment, joy, and love for the events of each and every day, even on the most challenging of days.

I have discovered that to be truly happy and to feel *alive* in life instead of just haphazardly living—existing—you must be willing to ask the question, "Who am I?" You must also be willing and courageous enough to search for the answers that will lead to the conscious creation of the life you want to live. Each and every moment brings with it possibilities and potential for a better life. No matter what, who, how, or where you think you are in your life right now, you can always aspire to better yourself, to better your life.

From conception, we have been consciously, subconsciously, and unconsciously developing and creating ourselves, and we will continue to do so for the rest of our lives. Humans grow and develop every moment, whether we are aware of it or not. We define and redefine who we are every moment as we choose our **E**motions, **A**ctions/behaviors, and **T**houghts (**EAT**s) that ultimately create and chart our journeys into our futures.

As human beings, we have the capacity to learn, create, and store information in order to build and establish who we are. Your life's history can be used as a personal magnifying glass to further your understanding of yourself, your surroundings, and your environment. The happenings of your day-to-day life hold all of the information that is needed to support you on your personal life journey to discover who you really are.

Although there are no promises of a quick fix in life, I have discovered that the clearest and most direct line to inner wisdom, clarity, and peace is self-communication through journaling. Many years of my own soul searching has led me to expressive journaling and the creation of *Me: Life Guide and Guided Journey by Journal*, which has transformed—and is still transforming—my life. This life guide and guided journal functions as a self-support system that will educate, motivate, and inspire you to generate more positive and wanted habits, balancing and creating your **EAT**s to guide you to the life you consciously want to create for yourself.

In addition to pertinent life facts and information found here, this guide includes an 11 week guided journal. The guided journal is composed of **7 Soul:Minds Exercises** that will support you in establishing more conscious and positive life habits. The self-awareness gained by self-communicating through journaling can be used as a tool to create more conscious awareness of the person you are right now and support and guide you to create and transform yourself into the person you con-sciously want to be.

Within 11 weeks, you can acquire **EAT**s that will support and guide you to create and instill conscious, subconscious, and unconscious chosen and wanted positive habits that will tremendously transform your life and the lives of those around you for the better.

Know thyself.
—SOCRATES (470—399 BC)

Self-Communication

> If you just communicate, you can get by.
> But if you communicate skillfully, you can work miracles.
> —JIM ROHN (1930—2009)

WHAT IS SELF-COMMUNICATION, AND HOW DO I CREATE IT?

com·mu·ni·cate[1]
(verb)

- share or exchange information, news, or ideas.
- impart or pass on (information, news, or ideas).
- convey or transmit (an emotion or feeling) in a nonverbal way.
- succeed in conveying one's ideas or in evoking understanding in others.

We all share a fundamental drive to communicate. It is one of the first—if not *the* first—thing we learn to do as human beings. Our ability to communicate is essential in order to get to know, understand, love, and relate better with others; our ability to self-communicate is especially important to get to know, understand, love, and relate better with the most important person in the world: you!

The discoveries you will make by self-communicating through journaling will support you to become more self-aware—revealing subconscious and unconscious patterns, bringing them into your consciousness, where they can be observed, examined, developed, and transformed.

---

1 All definitions referenced from *Google Dictionary.*

HOW CAN LEARNING SELF-COMMUNICATE SKILLS TRANSFORM MY LIFE?

Self-communication through journaling facilitates awareness of specific Emotions, Actions/behaviors, and Thoughts. It creates an access point for revealing and discovering the information that is necessary, preempting their examination and development. These are the fundamental steps in transforming specific EATs that are not working for you in your life into the EATs that will grant you the life you want to live. In my case, it was a life of hope, happiness, peace, and love.

I find that self-communication through guided expressive journaling provides a way for me to get to know myself by investigating, studying, and researching *me*. As I recorded my EATs on paper, I found that they opened a pathway for the discovery of *me*, and that is when I finally received the answers to all the questions I had been asking so many professionals for years. Discovering and embracing my inner strengths supports me in creating a happier, more loving, more hopeful, and more fulfilled life. It supplies me with the courage to face my fears and communicate with myself.

I began to ask myself questions by writing them down on paper, and then I found myself answering those same questions. I saved the pages. The answers served as evidence and as tools for self-development through self-reflection, self-discovery, and self-examination. Discovering who you are begins with asking yourself the question, "Who am I, really?" and finding the courage to search and investigate in order to discover the answers.

My personal journal liberates me. It is a platform that enables an internal dialogue with an external paper trail. In other words, it is a facilitator of self-communication and self-awareness. Expressive journaling allows me to acknowledge who I really am and to simply be *me*. It serves as a habitual support system that grants insight into my **E**motions, **A**ctions/behaviors, and **T**houghts in order for me to become aware of them and how they affect me and others. This form of introspection has freed me from my former perceptions of life. It has led me to the discovery of goals, dreams, and ambitions—my life's purpose, which ultimately were created and supported through the challenges I have encountered throughout my life and to this day.

> Without self-awareness we are as babies in the cradles.
> —Virginia Woolf (1882—1941)

Self-Awareness

WHAT IS SELF-AWARENESS, AND HOW DO I CREATE IT?

self-a·ware·ness
(noun)

- conscious knowledge of one's own character, feelings, motives, and desires.

Gathering and recording information about your specific **E**motions, **A**ctions/behaviors, and **T**houghts with this guided journal promotes and leads to greater self-awareness. Information is brought into your conscious mind, revealing unconscious **EAT**s. Once you become aware of them, transformation can take place. You can discover, examine, and develop yourself using the information you obtain from your own observations.

Remaining unconscious or unaware of your **EAT**s increases the chance that you will enter an unwanted loop or cycle of **E**motions, **A**ctions/behaviors, and **T**houghts. Self-awareness can transform unconscious loops/cycles. (More on the **EAT** Loop in chapter 2.)

Human Habits

Nothing is stronger than a habit.
Habits change into character.
—Ovid (43 BC—17/18 AD)

Human beings are creatures of habit. We all develop our own personal habits in order to construct and create our lives. We may not notice them on a regular basis, but we all possess habitual emotional, behavioral, and thought patterns. According to Charles Duhigg, author of *The Power of Habit*, habits are not born but created. Every bad, good, or insignificant habit starts with a psychological pattern called a habit loop.

HOW CAN BECOMING AWARE OF MY DAILY HABITS INFLUENCE MY LIFE?

Self-communication through guided journaling grants an access point that allows you to become more aware of your habit loops. Once discovered, they can be examined and, if need be, transformed to support the life you consciously choose to live. The self-awareness gained through habitually completing the **7 Soul:Minds Exercises** at the end of each day allows for the discovery of embedded beliefs and values, the sources of your habits. It is these very same beliefs and values that are the basis of every **E**motion you feel, **A**ction you take, and **T**hought you think and they are the same beliefs and values that are the basis of every **E**motion you don't feel, **A**ction you don't take and **T**hought you don't think. By discovering habitual **EAT**s through journaling, you create a passageway to the investigation, discovery, examination, transformation, and development of these very habits. In other words, observation and awareness of your habits allows you to consciously create your life as you choose.

Research has shown that it takes up to sixty-six days for a new behavior to become a habit.[2] Therefore, the **7 Soul:Minds Exercises** that make up the guided journal portion of this guide/journal are based on a question–answer exercise routine to be carried out at the end of each day for 11 weeks (seventy-seven days adding flexibility). Exercising your **Soul:Minds**, your three **Minds**: conscious, subconscious, and unconscious **Minds**, in this manner will influence, create, and establish positive, congruent **EATs**. The **7 Soul:Minds Exercises** strategically condition and prepare your brain before it downloads and stores influential information to memory in your conscious, subconscious, and unconscious **Minds** during sleep.[3] All the while, you are forming habits of learning that can significantly shape your present, create peace with your past, and transform your tomorrow.

2 Phillippa Lally et al., "How Are Habits Formed: Modeling Habit Formation in the Real World," *European Journal of Social Psychology*, 40, no. 6 (October 2010), https://doi.org/:10.1002/ejsp.674.
3 James Clear, "How Long Does It Actually Take to Form a New Habit? (Backed by Science)," *Huffington Post*, June 10, 2014, https://www.huffingtonpost.com/james-clear/forming-new-habits_b_5104807.html; Carolyn Gregoire, "5 Amazing Things Your Brain Does While You Sleep," *Huffington Post*, September 29, 2014, https://www.huffingtonpost.com/2014/09/28/brain-sleep-_n_5863736.html.

Conscious, Subconscious, and Unconscious Minds

WHAT ARE THE THREE MINDS, AND HOW DO THEY COMMUNICATE WITH EACH OTHER?

According to Sigmund Freud, within the human mind there exists three levels of awareness or consciousness. Freud's theory is that we use 10 percent of our conscious **Mind**, 50–60 percent of our subconscious **Mind**, and 30–40 percent of our unconscious **Mind**. Working together they create our reality.

The word **Minds** will be used throughout this guide when referring to all three levels of awareness or consciousness: conscious, subconscious and the unconscious **Minds**.

- The **conscious Mind** is the seat of logic, reasoning, focusing and imagination. By observing, paying attention to something, you spark the conscious **Mind**, becoming more aware of the source of your consciousness—the subconscious, and unconscious. The conscious **Mind**, combined with the other **Minds**, supplies you with the ability to complete many tasks at once—all while remaining aware of what is going on around you. For instance, you use your conscious **Mind**, along with other **Minds**, to assist you in performing tasks that are pertinent for observation such as driving, writing, exercising, studying, meditating, walking, and so on.
- The **subconscious Mind** allows for quick memory accessibility. For example, you use the subconscious **Mind** to recall phone numbers, multiplication tables, people's faces, and connecting faces to names, places, and events and how you have chosen to feel, act/behave, and think about those same people, places, things, and events through memories that have been stored in your **Minds**. The subconscious **Mind** acts as a mediator, a translator of the unconscious to the conscious **Mind** and vice versa (the conscious **Mind** to the unconscious **Mind**).

- The **unconscious Mind** is the grand memory database that maintains and communicates your created beliefs and values through your conscious and subconscious **Minds**. It is here that primal, instinctual **E**motions, **A**ctions/behaviors, and **T**houghts become memories, habits, patterns, attitudes, beliefs and values that are relayed through your subconscious **Mind** to your conscious **Mind**. The roots of your **EAT**s are based on what has been created and stored in your unconscious **Mind**; DNA, childhood and life experiences that have influenced you through your surroundings—namely, the people, places, things, events, and so on that have affected your life—are the platform you have built your **EAT**s on and have created and stored in your **Minds**.

Until you make the unconscious conscious,
it will direct your life and you will call it fate.
—CARL JUNG (1875—1961)

---※---

CHAPTER 2

You Are What You EAT

The EAT Loop

Diagram 1

Influential EATs

HOW DO MY EATS INFLUENCE ME?

EMOTIONS, ACTIONS/BEHAVIORS, AND Thoughts have been and will be mentioned quite a few times throughout this guide/journal. The repetition is intentional. It will instill them in your conscious, subconscious, and unconscious **Minds**.

You are what you **EAT**! Becoming aware of and granting expression to all of the **E**motions, **A**ctions/behaviors, and **T**houghts that arise creates clarity and promotes balance in life. After all, how would or could you know what happiness truly is if you never experienced sadness? Without sorrow, how would or could you truly experience joy? Without actions, behaviors, and words, how would or could you fully express yourself? Without thoughts, who would you be? Now, *there's* a thought!

Your **EAT**s are created by your beliefs and values. They influence one another, each entity transforming, developing and creating the next and their results create your life. They are the reality of every human being. Together, they hold the keys to unlocking who you are. They reveal the real "you," your authentic self, to you. Once you become aware, conscious of them, you can choose to transform them. This transformation process happens the moment your **EAT**s are observed, brought to your consciousness. Quantum theory supports this phenomenon. (More on quantum theory in chapter 6.)

Emotions

e·mo·tion
(noun)

- a natural instinctive state of mind deriving from one's circumstances, mood, or relationships with others.
- instinctive or intuitive feeling as distinguished from reasoning or knowledge.

Emotions are feelings that are experienced in response to **A**ctions/behaviors and **T**houghts created from your beliefs and values. **E**motions are made up of energy that is in motion and they influence your **A**ctions/behaviors and your **T**hought processes as well as create and strengthen your beliefs and values.

For example, from childhood, many of us may have been taught to repress certain emotions, even though experiencing a whole spectrum of emotions is crucial and empowering in our lives.

Hope cannot exist without hopelessness.
Happiness cannot exist without sadness.
Joy cannot exist without anger.
Satisfaction cannot exist without envy.
Courage cannot exist without cowardice.

It is not possible for an emotion to exist within you without the existence and personal knowledge of its opposite. Experiencing an entire spectrum of emotions/feelings is essential to recognizing and understanding the power of each one, and it is conducive to living an emotionally balanced and harmonious life. Conscious realization and expression of all of the emotions that exist within you will provide more clarity and freedom in your everyday life.

There are many ways to express our emotions. People feel and communicate them differently—uniquely—based on their life histories, what they have been taught, and what has been created and stored in their system of beliefs and values. The guided journey by journal found here will support you in the discovery and expression of your emotions.

Unexpressed emotions will never die.
They are buried alive and will come
forth later in uglier ways.
—Sigmund Freud (1856—1939)

Actions/behaviors

ac·tion
(noun)

- the fact or process of doing something, typically to achieve an aim.
- a thing done; an act.
- a manner or style of doing something, typically the way in which a mechanism works or a person moves.

Actions create behaviors. You act on your beliefs and values in many ways with the words you choose to use and the way you choose to use them, and with your behavior, facial expressions, tone of voice, and so on, in correspondence with your **T**houghts and **E**motions. Your **A**ctions/ behaviors influence your **E**motional and **T**hought processes and support, create, reinforce, and protect the beliefs and values that have been stored.

Behavior is a mirror in which everyone
displays his own image.
—Johann Wolfgang Von Goethe (1749—1832)

Thoughts

thought
(noun)

- an idea or opinion produced by thinking or occurring suddenly in the mind.
- the formation of opinions, especially as a philosophy or system of ideas, or the opinions so formed.
- careful consideration or attention.

Thoughts are created by your beliefs and values. They are the internal processing of the **A**ctions/behaviors and **E**motions that are connected with them. Your **T**houghts influence your **A**ctions/behaviors and **E**motions, as well as support, create, and strengthen your beliefs and values.

A man is but the product of his thoughts
what he thinks, he becomes.
—MAHATMA GANDHI (1869—1948)

Unconsciousness/unawareness of your **E**motions, **A**ctions/behaviors, and **T**houghts makes it more likely to get caught up in a loop that recycles unwanted **EAT**s. (Today, I realize that this is where *I* was for many years—unconsciously caught up in an unwanted **EAT** loop.) Self-awareness through investigation and discovery identifies **EAT**s. Identifying them furthers their transformation/development and enables you to create balance and harmony in your life all the while influencing the lives of those around you, your surroundings, for the better. Practicing what you consciously choose to **EAT** can create harmony and balance in any situation that happens *for* you in your life.

Watch your thoughts;
    they become your words.
Watch your words;
    they become your actions.
Watch your actions;
    they become your habits.
Watch your habits;
    they become your character.
Watch your character;
    it becomes your destiny.
      —LAO-TZU (604—531 BC)

Years later...

Carefully watch your thoughts,
    for they become your words.
Manage and watch your words,
    for they will become your actions.
Consider and judge your actions,
    for they have become your habits.
Acknowledge and watch your habits,
    for they shall become your values.
Understand and embrace your values,
    for they become your destiny.
      —MAHATMA GANDHI (1869—1948)

CHAPTER 3

Who Am I, Really?

The Spirit~Soul:Minds~Body~Environment Connection

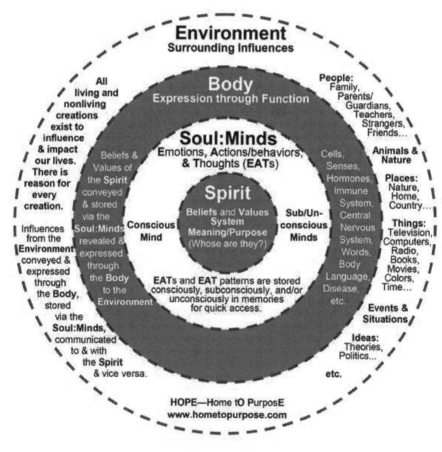

Diagram 2

YOUR SPIRIT~SOUL:MINDS~BODY~ENVIRONMENT ARE connected, and each entity influences and affects the next. Investigating and examining diagram 2, layer by layer, allows for more awareness and understanding of who you are and how you are created to grow and develop.

Your Spirit

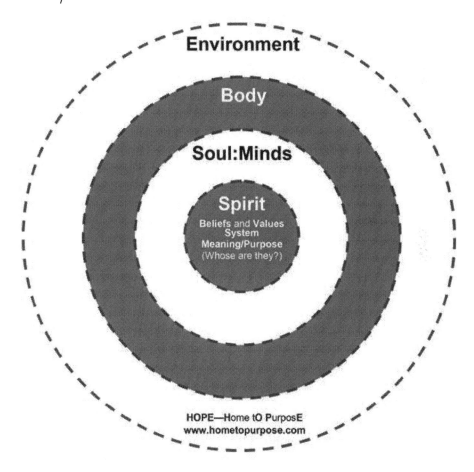

Diagram 2a

Your **Spirit**, your core, is your control center. It's home to your specific beliefs and values system, where each individual's meaning and purpose are stored, created, developed, and transformed by you.

Your **Spirit** communicates your core, your origins, to your three **Minds** (conscious, subconscious, and unconscious)—your **Soul:Minds**. Information is delivered from and by your **Spirit**—your specific beliefs and values system—and is relayed through your **Soul:Minds** to the cells that make up your **Body**, sending messages, communicating to and with your entire **Body** through your brain and nervous system, your central nervous system. This form of cellular communication reaches every part of your body—your muscles, tissues, organs, and so on.

Your **Body** receives the information and then expresses and communicates your specific beliefs, values, meaning, and purpose, revealing your **Spirit** to your **Environment**—and to you—through your **Spirit~Soul:Minds~ Body~Environment** connection.

HOW CAN I TRULY KNOW MYSELF AND BECOME AWARE OF THE BELIEFS AND VALUES THAT ARE STORED WITHIN MY SPIRIT?

The journey of knowing yourself, the discovery of who you really are, begins with taking the first step—stepping into self-awareness. Becoming aware of yourself, your beliefs, and your values and realizing that they are communicated to and through the specific **E**motions, **A**ctions/behaviors, and **T**houghts expressed through your **Body**, enables you to consciously create and choose the way you want to live. There is a way to step out of the state of unconsciousness—unawareness of your **EAT**s—and step into states of consciousness—consciously choosing to create and transform your **EAT**s. You create your reality. Self-awareness, knowing yourself, allows for greater learning and exploring of the beliefs and values that exist within you. The personal knowledge that you gain will assist and support you in the discovery and transformation of who you are and who you want to become.

The beliefs and values of your **Spirit** are the core of every **E**motion you feel, every **A**ction you take, and every **T**hought you think, remember? Investigating the what, how, when, where, and why of each **EAT** allows for self-development through self-awareness. Use your **EAT**s as guides to further greater and more defined self-communication skills.

Your Soul:Minds

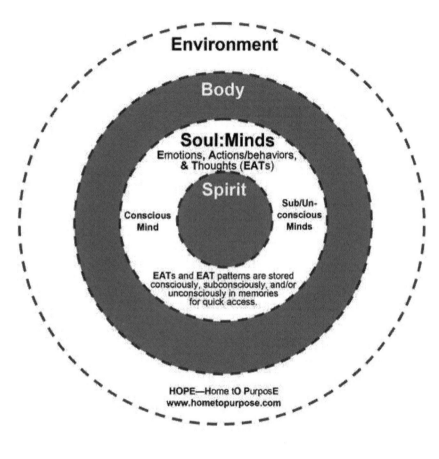

Diagram 2b

Your **Soul:Minds** are also known as your conscious, subconscious, and unconscious **Minds**; they store your chosen **EATs**.

Involuntary, subconscious, and/or unconscious bodily functions—such as the pumping of your heart, blood flow regulation, breathing, body temperature regulation, and so much more—are conducted by and through your **Soul:Minds**. These actions are involuntary and unconscious—thank goodness for that! If it were left up to you to voluntarily and consciously breathe or make your heart beat, when and how could you ever rest? Just as your **Body** has involuntary, unconscious actions, you are also capable of voluntary, conscious actions—actions of choice. For example, you can choose to hold your breath or to raise your heart rate and blood pressure through aerobic exercise.

Understanding the functioning of the **Body** reveals many outstanding examples of life energy and life force, which will be discussed further in chapter 4.

Your **Soul:Minds** act as a communication barrier between your **Environment**, your **Body**, and your **Spirit**. It secures, maintains, and protects the beliefs, values, meaning, and purpose that are stored, created, developed, and transformed within the **Spirit**. It does this by storing **EAT**s that can be accessed quickly in order to relay, strengthen and/or protect, and reinforce the specific beliefs and values you have chosen to create in your **Spirit**.

Have you ever felt angry or frustrated because someone said or did something that was against your beliefs or values? Have you ever felt happy and/or more confident when someone said or did something that was in line with your beliefs and values? What actions did you take? What thoughts were running through your **Minds**? Awareness of what is happening *for* you in the moment will allow you to understand who you are at your core. Once you are aware, you can consciously choose to transform yourself into who you want to be.

Many of your **E**motions, **A**ctions/behaviors, and **T**houghts have been cultivated and stored to your **Minds**, your memories, your cells through your **Spirit** (meaning/purpose, beliefs, and values). DNA, childhood experiences, and factors seemingly beyond your control influenced and may still to this day influence your **Spirit**. By becoming more aware of your **EAT**s each day, you have the power to choose how you want to transform and develop yourself—thus, creating your life. The **EAT**s that have been stored in your **Soul:Minds** can be transformed by you and in turn they will transform your **Spirit**. It takes awareness, patience, and practice/habit, but you can most definitely **EAT,** believe, and value as you consciously choose.

Life happens *for* you, but you and only you choose your **EAT**s, beliefs, and values.

In the discovery of who you are, your **Soul:Minds** play a major role. It is here that you are able to become more aware of your **E**motions, **A**ctions/behaviors, and **T**houghts. By using what you have learned from the discoveries of your **EAT**s, you will obtain the very evidence needed to discover and understand the specific beliefs and values that have been created and stored within your **Spirit**—who you are at your core. Your **Soul:Minds** direct and guide you to where, what, when, how, and why you feel, act/behave, and think at any given moment per your specific beliefs and values system, your **Spirit**. It is here, through the **Soul:Minds** entity, you can become more aware of the beliefs and values that are stored in your **Spirit**.

Your **Soul:Minds** are intertwined. The key to life's transformation is acknowledging and understanding that **E**motions, **A**ctions/behaviors, and **T**houghts stored in your **Soul:Minds**—your conscious, subconscious, and unconscious—are dynamic; each one influences and affects the other.

Your Body

Diagram 2c

Scientists have discovered that humans are composed of more than 30 trillion cells that are busy at work for us 24/7.[4] Human beings begin the journey of life from two cells, one from an ovary and one from a sperm. These cells meet and unite to create one cell—you. This particular cell has multiplied and multiplied and multiplied over and over again, creating your nervous system, muscles, and organs such as the heart, brain, lungs,

---

4 E. Bianconi et al., "An Estimation of the Number of Cells in the Human Body," *Annals of Human Biology* 40, no. 6 (2013): 463–471, https://doi: 10.3109/03014460.2013.807878; Yella Hewings-Martin, "How Many Cells Are in the Human Body?" *Medical News Today*, July 12, 2017, https://www.medicalnewstoday.com/articles/318342.php.

and bones—in short, your entire **Body**. We humans also possess the ability to use our bodily senses—sight, hearing, smell, taste, and touch—by which we perceive stimuli originating from outside or from inside the **Body**. Senses act as a communication barrier between the **Body** and its surroundings, its **Environment**.

Research has taught us that the functioning of most cells that make up our body—for example, our organs and tissues—is controlled by the central nervous system (the control center and storage medium) located in the brain and spinal cord. Most of the time, we are unaware of the actions that occur—that is, they happen through our unconscious mind; they are involuntary actions.[5]

Via cells, your **Body** relays vital information about your **Spirit** to you and your **Environment** communicating the **E**motions, **A**ctions/behaviors, and **T**houghts of your **Soul:Minds.** Your **Body** broadcasts vital information about your **Spirit** (beliefs, values, meaning, and purpose) to you and your surroundings. Your physical and mental **Body** (cells) express your **Spirit** in many ways—through language, the words you choose to use and the way you choose to use them; your posture; your mental health; and your physical health via your immune system, hormone system, and so on. Via your senses and other bodily functions, the cells that make up your **Body** come together and act as an interface between the **EAT**s that are stored in your **Soul:Minds** and the beliefs and values that are stored in your **Spirit**. These are then relayed to you and your **Environment**/surroundings and vice versa. This system works both ways: from the inside out and from the outside in, a concept that will be further explained in the summary.

---

5 "How Does the Nervous System Work? Informed Health Online," *PubMed Health*, August 19, 2016, https://www.ncbi.nlm.nih.gov/pubmedhealth/PMH0072574/.

Your Environment

Environment
Surrounding Influences

Body

Soul:Minds

Spirit

All living and nonliving creations exist to influence & impact our lives. There is reason for every creation.

Influences from the Environment conveyed & expressed through the Body, stored via the Soul:Minds, communicated to & with the Spirit & vice versa.

People: Family, Parents/ Guardians, Teachers, Strangers, Friends...

Animals & Nature

Places: Nature, Home, Country...

Things: Television, Computers, Radio, Books, Movies, Colors, Time...

Events & Situations

Ideas: Theories, Politics...

etc.

HOPE—Home tO PurposE
www.hometopurpose.com

Diagram 2d

Your **Environment**, your surroundings, is made up of all of the living and nonliving creations that influence your life—people, places, things, ideas, events, situations, television shows, movies, magazines, advertisements, news, politics, nature, weather, animals, colors, numbers, and so on.

From conception until this day, your **Environment** has played and still plays a major role in the creation of who you are. Becoming more aware of your surroundings, your **Environment**, will shed more light on your day-to-day influences and specific habits that you are unconsciously perfecting and instilling in your **Spirit.**

Summary

SPIRIT~SOUL:MINDS~BODY~ENVIRONMENT CONNECTION

Your **Spirit**, your core, the home of your meaning and purpose in life, communicates information from your beliefs and values system, which forms the patterns of **E**motions, **A**ctions/behaviors, and **T**houghts in your **Soul:Minds** (the conscious, subconscious, and unconscious **Minds**). Your **Soul:Minds** deliver the specific **EAT**s that will be performed and relayed through the cells of your **Body** at any given time in response to your **Environment**. All entities work together voluntarily and involuntarily to express who you are.

ENVIRONMENT~BODY~SOUL:MINDS~SPIRIT CONNECTION

Influences from the **Environment** relayed through human senses and expressions of the **Body** are communicated to your **Soul:Minds.** Your **Soul:Minds** process the **EAT**s that are received through your body and store pertinent information into memories of your **Minds**. Your **Minds**, your **Soul**, communicates with your **Spirit**, and choices are made to accept, dismiss, and hold for further processing as the **EAT**s are being transmitted and communicated. All the while influencing, creating, transforming, and strengthening—developing the beliefs and values system of your **Spirit**, where your individual meaning and purpose in life can be discovered.

In short, you are your **Body~Soul:Minds~Spirit**. These dynamic entities are influenced through your **Environment**/surroundings, but the ultimate choice is yours to make. You can discover who you really are by performing a self-investigation and becoming more aware of yourself. By identifying who you have become in this moment, you are more able to consciously choose how you want to live your life, who you want to be and the transformations you would like to make.

Gravity

WHAT DOES GRAVITY HAVE TO DO WITH MY SPIRIT~SOUL:MINDS~ BODY~ENVIRONMENT CONNECTION?

According to Wikipedia, gravity, or gravitation, is a natural phenomenon by which all things with mass are brought toward (or *gravitate* toward) one another, including objects ranging from atoms and photons to planets and stars. Because energy and mass are equivalent, all forms of energy (including light) cause gravitation and are under the influence of it.

Gravity influences the entire universe, and you, your **Spirit**, are influenced by what is gravitated toward and away from you. Your **Spirit** communicates your meaning, purpose, beliefs, and values with your **Environment**, the universe, through the specific **EAT**s that are relayed to the cells of your **Body** in order to express your **Spirit** through it. Your **Spirit** acts as a magnet and a compass, guiding you toward and away from the specific people, places, things, and events in order to further your individual choices, growth, and developmental processes, allowing you to become more aware of who you are by revealing what is stored in your **Spirit** at any given moment. Your **Spirit** acts as a magnet in the same way as gravity does, drawing toward you what you consciously or unconsciously believe and value and have stored within your **Spirit**. Your **Spirit** attracts and repels using your beliefs and values as the guide for everything that is gravitated toward and away from you.

LIFE HAPPENS *FOR* YOU AND GRAVITY *SUPPORTS* LIFE

The ability to become more conscious/aware of and grateful for your specific life happenings will allow you to make choices that will support you in order to define and transform your history—your past, your present, and your future.

Human beings support and influence one another in our individual life journeys, whether we are aware of it or not. You are surrounded by and gravitate toward and away from the specific people, places, things, ideas, events, and so on, according to the beliefs and values stored, created, developed, transformed, and strengthened in your **Spirit**. Consciousness of this phenomenon grants you the power of choice, allowing you to choose how and what is gravitated toward you and away from you.

We are all on a common journey. We are all made up of cells that are living, multiplying, and dying. We all influence one another *for a reason*—to support one another in becoming aware of ourselves and our **Environments** in order to fulfill our life's purpose.

Take a good look around you and
listen closely with your heart;
THE UNIVERSE IS TRYING TO TELL YOU SOMETHING.

C H A P T E R   4

Life's Purpose

The purpose of life is to live a life of purpose.
—Robert Byrne (1930—2016)

What is the purpose of human life?

pur·pose
(noun)

- the reason for which something is done or created or for which something exists.
- have as one's intention or objective.

Life is abundant. It can be found everywhere you look.

Life and energy, *life's energy*, is pumping your heart, supporting you in taking your next breath—keeping you alive. Life has a purpose. All of these amazing phenomena and more allow for life to continue, to evolve. They exist for a reason, meaning they do not just haphazardly happen.

The author Mark Twain wrote, "The two most important days in your life are the day you are born and the day you find out why."

For most of my life, I have pondered the question of why. *Why me? Why was I born into this world? Is there a meaning to life; is there a purpose?*

What I have discovered through journaling, self-communication, and investigation is that every moment of every day brings with it the opportunity to find out why we were born. There are no secrets to knowing and understanding who you are. Simply learning about yourself and consciously creating and transforming yourself from what you have learned, day-by-day, using the happenings of your life as a reference point, will supply you with your answers. Twain couldn't have summed it up better. Each day that encompasses awareness, self-knowledge, and support to further transformational and developmental life processes is an important day.

Live in the moment—in your now—and learn from it.

I am also quite aware that the more I know and understand, the more I realize that there is so much more to know and understand about life, about my life. Life is more complex than we can conceive or perceive, but thanks to journaling, I am more aware of my beliefs and values, and I can wholeheartedly proclaim the following to be true:

I believe that our greatest purpose in life is to live each and every moment with an inner harmony, a harmony within our **Spirit, Soul:Minds**, and **Body** that radiates out and influences our **Environment**. Creating this level of harmony entails learning about who we are in this moment, accepting ourselves without self-flagellation, and **loving ourselves unconditionally** every moment of every day.

Unconditional Love

In my experience of asking people what they *want* in their lives, their top four choices are **happiness**, **health**, **loving relationships**, and **wealth**. The most fascinating discoveries that you will make while journeying by journal using the **7 Soul:Minds Exercises** found later in this guide are that you can receive all four of these choices and more. Simply by learning to love who you are, loving what you already possess, and loving yourself in every single moment that life gifts to you, no matter what the circumstances are in that moment, you create all four of the above and more.

Possessing unconditional self-love—"true love"—is the support needed to learn from and develop yourself throughout your life. By acquiring the knowledge and understanding of true love created from within, **happiness** and security will be abundant, and you will be more able to share that love unconditionally with others, without expectations or judgments.

Self-love is accompanied with the knowledge and understanding that you are worthy and unique. When you truly love yourself, you consciously **choose** to love and take care of the body you live in. Self-sabotage will begin to diminish, and you will choose to become aware of, create, and develop physical and mental **healthy lifestyle habits**, such as improving your nutrition, exercise, and sleep habits, as well as your **E**motional, **A**ction/behavioral, and **T**hinking habits. Your **Environment**/surroundings will also become more important to you.

In loving yourself unconditionally, you create, know, and understand what a **loving relationship** is all about firsthand. You will always be loved, and you will never be alone, because you will always have yourself—you are the only person who can "self-love" you. No one or thing can do it for you. Trust me, I've tried! I've paid humungous sums of money in the search for "me," and I have discovered that others can support, inspire, influence, and even spark your motivation, but you are the only one who can truly help you!

No One Knows You Better Than You Know Yourself.

As for **wealth**, self-love will grant you all of the above, and you will discover riches and fortunes in your life that money simply cannot buy.

HOW DO I LOVE MYSELF UNCONDITIONALLY?

Many of us are quick to remember our problems, shortcomings, and weaknesses, and we are slow, if not stagnant, in practicing the remembrance of our accomplishments, gifts, and strengths. Most of us have a tendency to become judgmental and critical of ourselves and therefore fail to apply unconditional self-love, which is the opposite of self-judgment and self-criticism. Unconditional self-love is loving yourself precisely as you are right now, in this moment, no matter what. It is learning about, forgiving, and accepting yourself while evolving and transforming. It is this love that creates compassion and kindness for your unique self. There is only one of you, and there will never be another like you—EVER. You are truly special.

The ability to love yourself unconditionally radiates outward to your surroundings, allowing you to love, learn from, forgive, and accept the people, places, things, and events that supported, support, and will support you in the creation of who you are throughout your lifetime. When you can honestly and truly love yourself in any situation, you are more able to share that love with others. Possessing self-love is the basis of all love.

Life Happens FOR a Reason

Today, I am more aware, and I endeavor to learn, grow, and develop from the people, places, things, and events that occur and have occurred for me every moment of every day of my life. I do this with the belief that everything happens *for* a reason. Life does not happen *to* me; rather, life happens *for* me. It happens *for* me to learn, grow, and develop. Life happens on purpose, *for* a purpose.

Realizing and believing that life happens *for* you will grant the support you'll need to unravel your specific life mysteries. It will allow you to further understand, forgive, love, and be grateful for every moment that brings with it the gift of life. Life as you know it exists for you to learn, grow, and develop in self-love. That is the ultimate purpose of your life and of all of our lives.

Life is always happening *for* you, *for* a purpose.

Every Creation Has a Purpose

Every person, every place, every event—everything—has a purpose, whether we can understand and comprehend the purpose or not. All living and nonliving creations exist to influence and impact our lives. We may not always be able to comprehend why certain things happen in our lives, but life certainly happens **for** us, **for** us to grow and develop.

Life is full of ups and downs. Our world is made up of good and bad, darkness and light, sickness and health, birth and death, success and failure, and so on. They all must exist; every one of them serves a purpose. Knowledge of one enables knowledge of the other. Each one is necessary for its opposite to exist. Appreciating, learning from and using your knowledge of them *all* enable you to create more balance and personal harmony in your individual life.

Choosing to search and discover who you really are on your unique life's journey by becoming aware of and grateful for all of life's happenings will equip you with the inner strength and knowledge to balance yourself and bring harmony into your life.

Power of Choice/Free Will and Inner Strength/Willpower

HOW CAN UNDERSTANDING THE CONCEPT OF FREE WILL AND WILLPOWER STRENGTHEN MY AWARENESS ABILITIES AND TRANSFORM MY LIFE?

Nothing can stand in the way of your personal inner strength/willpower and free will. They are a prerequisite for establishing habits, and therefore they are needed in the process of exercising your conscious, subconscious, and unconscious **Minds** (your **Soul:Minds**) creating awareness that will transform your life.

Your free will grants you the power to choose, and willpower defines, shapes, and strengthens your choice into a habit, part of your life.

Many people have come to believe that their power of choice/free will has been taken away from them. They believe that certain people, places, things, and events in their lives were chosen for them and that they had absolutely no choice in the matter. At the time of the happening, this may have seemed true. But many of these same people have habitually chosen—using their own free will and willpower, consciously and/or sub/unconsciously—to **relive** and **remember** the bad, the wrong, the worst, and the pain in their lives. With time, this habit becomes encrypted and stored in the beliefs and values system of their **Spirits**.

I have yet to meet a person whose life has remained unscathed by people, places, things, and/or events. Life happens. Life happens *for* us, and every moment of our lives is necessary in order to support our unique and individual growth and development processes. Every moment of our lives empowers us to use our free will to accept, transform, and create ourselves as we choose. We are definitely influenced by our **Environment**s—past, present, and future—but it is *we* who choose how *we* will **EAT**. We create our realities. Jimmy Dean was quoted as saying, "I can't change the direction of the wind, but I can adjust my sails to always reach my destination."

Free will enables you to choose how you live your life. Who you are at this moment in time is dependent on how you chose and still choose to **E**motion/feel, **A**ct/behave, and **T**hink about those very same people, places, things, and events that influence your life. You and only you are able to choose your **EAT**s, no matter how you were raised and what you were taught through your **Environment**, your surroundings.

What has happened in the past is history, and from history, we can only learn.

Using your free will, your power of choice, to look for the good in everything in your life will propel you to become a better you—a person that **you** are happy to be with and love without condition. How you live your life is, indeed, your creation and your choice.

Things happened, happen, and will happen in your life. Searching deep within yourself to find the good that comes from and with every person, every place, everything, and every event that happens **for** you in life is the key to leading a free, hopeful, peaceful, joyful, and loving life.

We *are* living in a good universe, and every moment brings the ability to discover the good that comes from our lives. The alternative is to confine ourselves to a downtrodden perception of life. Every moment brings with it the ability to become more self-aware, which in turn allows us to make more conscious positive life choices.

Free will is a gift that we all possess. It is enabling you to choose to read these words right now. By becoming aware of and using this gift, you have the power to create and transform yourself, your life. The final call is yours. Life is your choice, your creation. However you choose to live it, **it is your life**.

Life truly is as easy—and as difficult—as you perceive it to be. You alone create the way **you** live **your** life. It's your reality.

Life Traumas

LIFE IS ALWAYS HAPPENING ON PURPOSE, FOR A REASON, FOR YOU

Many people are conflicted when it comes to the understanding and comprehension of the statements *life happens* **for** *you, life happens* **for** *a reason, life happens on purpose,* and so on. How would or could you explain these statements to the parents of innocent children with life-threatening diseases, rape victims, or war and natural disasters victims? How in the world could any of these traumatizing, life-altering events happen *for* anyone?

A few things we all can be sure of is that we are alive, life *happens*, and life evolves. Our lives are influenced by the people, places, things, and events that surround us. At the end of the day, how each of us, individually, chooses to evolve by way of our **E**motions, **A**ctions/behaviors, and **T**houghts is definitely a choice we each make for ourselves, consciously and/or unconsciously. In a single moment, a traumatic event can affect and influence your life and the lives of others, but as we evolve and grow, those moments and what we have chosen to **E**motion, **A**ct/behave, and **T**hink about them also evolves within us and can influence our evolution and the evolution of those around us.

Life happens whether we like it or not. Our ultimate combined goal in life is to hold the belief that we live in a good universe and that everything happened, happens, and will happen *for* a reason, whether we are aware of that reason or not.

Each of us lives our specific life happenings, and as individuals, we create our own fluctuating levels of **E**motions/feelings, **A**ctions/behaviors, and **T**houghts, which are influenced by those specific happenings. With our uniqueness comes misunderstanding. How could we ever really understand someone else? We are all unique. We can never place ourselves in someone else's shoes and be that person. It is not possible. We can try, and sometimes we get really close to understanding—on the same page, so to speak—but in the end, we are all different even though we have so much in common.

The desire to support fellow humans and ourselves in an effort to show compassion and kindness by taking care of and sharing our love for ourselves and others in times of happiness and in times of hardship is a wonderful, shared human quality. By supporting others in times of hardship, we are not only reminded of our own hardships, but we are also given the choice to ease our own pain and suffering by becoming more aware of our **EAT**s as we support others. By celebrating with others in times of happiness, we are reminded of and create more happiness within ourselves. This is true for all **EAT**s of fear, jealousy, anger, hate, resentment, love, contentment, joy, kindness, forgiveness, and so on. When they are practiced and exercised repeatedly, we create, develop, and strengthen more of the same within ourselves. The happenings of our lives that affect our **EAT**s the most are the ones that we learn and develop from the most.

Personal Hidden Trauma

Keeping personal traumas quiet, hidden deep inside and not communicated, is like tiptoeing through a minefield afraid and worried that at any moment, you could step on a trigger and ignite even more trauma. Becoming aware of, discovering, and learning about yourself; loving yourself *no matter what*; and finding the good that comes from all people, places, things, and events that happened, happen, and will happen *for* you in your individual life, *no matter what*, will defuse any bomb that has been set and is ticking.

A deep cut in your skin that is ignored and left uncared for has the potential to eventually become infected and can infect your entire body. But if properly cared for, it will heal. Human instinct and the teachings of life prompt us to clean and care for the wound until it heals. In the moments after sustaining a deep cut, the reason(s) why you were cut is/are irrelevant. It has already happened. Paying attention to and caring for your wound is of the utmost importance. It will promote the healing process.

Caring for yourself enough to apply unconditional self-love throughout the happenings of your life will allow for more self-knowledge through self-communication. This will further your self-awareness, which can supply you with the ability to heal yourself and find balance and harmony in your life.

Discovering the good that accompanies all people, places, things, events, and situations in your life will ease the pain and promote healing from within. *Yes, good does come from every wound.* An example of the apparently *good* that comes from the apparently *bad* is people coming together and sharing their love for others by comforting distraught family members after a tragedy. Another is complete strangers suddenly appearing and giving of themselves to support another human being, an animal, or nature, and so on. Yet another example is being grateful for, appreciating and celebrating life and the time you had with the people, places, things, events, and situations that have influenced your life to this day and have passed on, or are no longer physically or materialistically in your life.

The so-called *bad* that accompanies you in your life supplies you with more opportunities to share your love with others and with yourself, and for others to share their love with you. Where in your life do you give of yourself without reason? If you look deep enough, you will always find that there is a reason, because life happens *for* a reason.

Believing that everything exists for a reason and has a purpose and that reason/purpose is positive, promoting growth and development, is a mind-set. It takes practice. Investigating to reveal the good that comes along with the comforts and discomforts, traumas and triumphs of life will bring peace and balance not only to your life but to the lives of others as well. Inability to discover the *good* in the happenings of your life only feeds and nourishes the *bad*, allowing it to grow and develop within you prolonging your personal pain and suffering that influences not only you, but also your surroundings. Whether you are aware of it or not, your personal suffering, as well as your personal pleasure, radiates outward to influence and affect your family, friends, surroundings, and our universe as a whole.

There is a purpose for your life—your conception, your life up until this moment, and every moment hereafter. As you grow and develop, awareness of your current **EAT**s will support you and guide you in the discovery of who you really are. They will provide insight into your individual life's purpose and give meaning to your life.

Searching for who you really are using books, workshops, lectures, and therapists or other professionals are all wonderful warm-ups, but the true training and transformation comes from within you. It comes from what you choose to *do* with it all, with all that influences you. Practice, exercise, and repetition make all the difference in forming life habits. By *doing*— taking action in your life—you can create and transform it into the life you want and consciously choose to live.

I believe that every single event in life happens
in an opportunity to choose love over fear.
—OPRAH WINFREY

Practice Perfects

WHAT AM I PRACTICING IN MY LIFE? WHAT AM I GETTING REALLY GOOD AT?

Perfection exists, as we are all perfect in our own uniqueness. Each person is special and perfect to humankind and to the universe exactly as they are in this moment. Who you have become up until now and who you, consciously and/or unconsciously, decide to be in every moment hereafter is your choice.

In life, we all practice many things—how to walk and talk; how to be in and out of a relationship; how to be a friend, a companion, a family member; how to make money; and how to love. We practice what makes us happy, sad, resentful, forgiving, angry, kind, and so on.

Consciousness of your practices/habits can provide you with an access point to create and build on what you really want and choose for yourself, for your life. You are your **E**motions, **A**ctions/behaviors, and **T**houghts, and they are created by and from your practices, which eventually form your life habits.

What is it that you are practicing? Is it fear, anger, worry, sadness, complaining, and jealousy? Is it love, peace, joy, happiness, contentment, and satisfaction? Are you practicing impatience or patience? What are you getting really good at? What are you perfecting?

Daily journaling creates awareness of your practices and of your habits. Guided daily journaling with the **7 Soul:Minds Exercises** can establish, strengthen, and develop practices that lead to habits that you consciously want for yourself and for your life.

We are what we repeatedly do.
Excellence, then, is not an act but a habit.
—ARISTOTLE

**Life skills are created through practice.
You are what you repeatedly EAT (Emotion, Act and Think).**

CHAPTER 5

Self-Identity

I am the only person in the world
I should like to know thoroughly.
—OSCAR WILDE (1854—1900)

Have I Identified (ID'ED) Who I Really Am?

i·den·ti·fy
(verb)

- to establish or indicate who or what (someone or something) is.

TRUE SELF-IDENTITY COMES through your ability to

Investigate to
Discover and
Examine who you really are in order to
Develop into who you want to be

using your **EAT**s as guides.

Have I **I**nvestigated to **D**iscover, **E**xamine, and **D**evelop my **E**motions, **A**ctions, and **T**houghts?

Have I **ID'ED** my **EAT**s?

Have I ID'ED My EATs?

HOW DO I INVESTIGATE TO DISCOVER, EXAMINE, AND DEVELOP MY TRUE IDENTITY?

Investigate Yourself

> What I am looking for is not out there; it is in me.
> —HELEN KELLER (1880—1968)

in·ves·ti·gate
(verb)

- carry out a systematic or formal inquiry to discover and examine the facts of (an incident, allegation, etc.) so as to establish the truth.
- make inquiries as to the character, activities, or background of (someone).

HOW DO I INVESTIGATE MYSELF?

A self-investigation or an internal investigation is the discovery of personal information using your **E**motions, **A**ctions/behaviors, and **T**houghts as the evidence that will ultimately reveal your true identity. Sound familiar?

Information/evidence is brought to your consciousness/awareness and ultimately used in facilitating self-development and living your *authentic* life—the life you were born to live. The tools are right under your nose, and the clues are all around you. At this moment, a magnifying glass has been placed in your hands. The question is, are you willing to look through it and begin to discover and examine yourself to become more aware of who you are and of your surroundings?

I have discovered an entity living inside me that I was not aware of, a factory of **E**motions, **A**ctions/behaviors, and **T**houghts that are produced whether I am aware of them or not. Each one supports and strengthens the others. At the core, the power source for this factory is my system of embedded beliefs and values. These same beliefs and values motivate and inspire my **EAT**s, which are discoverable through investigation.

Journaling plays a major role in self-investigation. By logging your **EAT**s, you are granted access to hidden information that can be used as evidence of the repetitive patterns in your life. Using this repetition as evidence to be examined will support you to identify who you are and provide you with the leverage to develop yourself as you choose.

Example: For many years, I wasn't aware that I chose sorrow and anger as my go-to emotions, although I did feel an emotional sorrow and anger in my life that stemmed from childhood and certain events that seemed to happen for no apparent reason at the time. That sorrow and anger led me to act and behave in a way that reflected emotions of sorrow and anger. I blamed others. I blamed my parents, my brothers, myself, and my **Environment**—others. This action/behavior led me to think that if this is the meaning of life, then it is not worth living. Why is life so hard? Why is this happening *to* me?

Back then, it didn't cross my mind to sit down with a pen and paper, write these questions down, and actually begin to answer them. I left them open-ended—as statements rather than questions—and this habit only reinforced my **E**motions of sorrow, sadness, and hopelessness; my **A**ctions of sorrow, blaming, judging, and criticizing others; and my **T**hinking that if this is the meaning of life, it is not worth living. Now I understand why I didn't want to get out of bed in the morning to relive it all over again.

For years, this was happening, and where was I? I was unconscious. I was not aware of it. I was caught up in a habitual **EAT** loop. These **EAT**s had been created, cultivated, and imprinted by me into my **Body**, **Soul:Minds**, and **Spirit** through my **Environment**/surroundings from conception.

Later in life, as an adult, I physically moved myself and my belongings to another country, but I could still feel the repercussions of my former **Environment**/surroundings. There is no hiding from your **Spirit**. It follows you wherever you go. It is encrypted, etched within you. I knew something was not right. I felt it. I didn't know what to do, so I continued my outward search for the answers, spending more of my time and money in the search for the person, place, or thing (I bought a lot of clothes and shoes back then) that would release and free me. By ignoring and/or not discovering the source of my inner **E**motions, **A**ctions/behaviors, and **T**houghts, I unknowingly enabled the **EAT** loop to repeat, supporting it and unconsciously letting it strengthen itself over and over for most of my life (see **EAT** diagram 1).

The most phenomenal thing about the **EAT** process is that being *aware* (conscious) of it or not being aware (unconscious) of it, it happens anyway. Awareness through investigation, discovery, examination, and development are essential to creating a conscious transformation, consciously choosing the life you **want** to live.

Conducting a self-investigation—an internal investigation through journaling—allows you to observe yourself and your **Environment** and brings awareness to your **EAT** loop. That awareness allows you to transform one or more of the loop's components, and by habitually doing so, you transform the entire loop. When you are aware of your **EAT**s, you are able to examine them and then choose how to transform and develop them. These are **the answers** from within.

Discover Yourself

The greatest discovery you will ever make in your life is self-discovery.

dis·cov·er
(verb)

- find (something or someone) unexpectedly or in the course of a search.
- become aware of (a fact or situation).
- be the first to find or observe (a place, substance, or scientific phenomenon).

Discovery is made possible through investigation. What is not sought after will go undiscovered. In general, investigators inquire, observe, and examine to gather information and develop their cases. By applying the same strategies, you are able to investigate to identify, observe, and examine who you really are and develop yourself. It is possible to **discover** your true identity by becoming a private investigator into your own personal **E**motions, **A**ctions/behaviors, and **T**houghts.

HOW DO I DISCOVER WHO I REALLY AM?

How do you acquaint yourself with loved ones, friends, and people in general? You ask them questions and you observe them. You get interested in *them*, and by doing so, you gather information. Lines of communication are opened, and a relationship forms. Communication is the expression of **E**motions, **A**ctions, and **T**houghts. By communicating your **EAT**s through journaling, you can observe yourself. You can get to know, love, and accept others by getting to know, love, and accept yourself.

Once you have **discovered** or become aware of a reoccurring **E**motion, **A**ction, or **T**hought, it/they can be **examined** to enhance your personal development.

Examine Yourself

The unexamined life is not worth living.
—SOCRATES (470—399 BC)

ex·am·ine
(verb)

- inspect (someone or something) in detail to determine their nature or condition; investigate thoroughly.
- test the knowledge or proficiency of (someone) by requiring them to answer questions or perform tasks.

Many of the feelings, actions, behaviors, thoughts, beliefs, and values that you possess today were cultivated, developed, learned, and encrypted within you by others. They were taught to you through your **Environment**/surroundings: your parents/guardians, teachers, and any persons, places, things, events, or situations that influenced and influence your life up until this very moment.

It is also important to remember that the very same people who influenced your life were also influenced by others. Many of their beliefs, values, **E**motions, **A**ctions/behaviors, and **T**houghts were cultivated, created, developed, learned, and encrypted by their parents/guardians, their teachers, their **Environment**/surroundings, and the people, places, things, events, and situations that influenced *their* lives up until that very moment.

Every generation influences and creates the next.

How Are You Raising Yourself?

At some point in life, you become the guardian of yourself. You grow up, develop, and begin to raise yourself. You have learned much about life. You have grown and have lived through your own personal triumphs and traumas, and you are still growing and living them. Use that knowledge to discover the good that comes from every situation and use it for your own good. Use it to raise yourself to your advantage, the way you choose.

The purpose of this guided journal is to create awareness of the cycles that are formed from generation to generation and individually. In this process, you will discover who **you** really are and choose to become who **you** want to be by strengthening, creating and/or transforming your **EAT**s.

I believe everything that happened, happens, and will happen in my life was, is, and will be *for* me.

Remember: Life happens *for* you, *for* a reason.

Develop Yourself

The ability to consciously develop oneself in love is the ultimate goal of every human being.

de·vel·op
(verb)

- grow or cause to grow and become more mature, advanced, or elaborate.
- start to exist, experience, or possess.

The information that is discovered can be examined through investigating the **E**motions, **A**ctions/behaviors, and **T**houghts that exist within you and then processed in order to develop and transform your life. Personal examination brings with it awareness, and it is this awareness that leads us to our personal willpower in order to develop and transform ourselves. In other words, awareness of your **EAT**s allows you to choose how you really want to live your life and develop appropriately.

Example: Once, I thought that I was not able, not strong enough to investigate or communicate with myself. I thought that the communication—the search and discovery—would take the little strength I had left to survive. I thought it would destroy me. I was afraid of what I might discover about myself. I was afraid that I would totally lose the little control I had left. Those thoughts influenced my actions/behavior—I chose to stay in bed in the morning, which in turn influenced my emotions and caused me to feel lifeless like a robot on autopilot, going through the motions. I felt useless, empty, and fragile, all of which reinforced the thought that I was not capable of investigating/searching for who I really was. For years, I chose to allow this **EAT** loop, this cycle, to continue because I was afraid to face it and I had gotten used to it. It was all I could do at the time. My habit, my practice, was corrosive and infectious, but it was comfortable—no unexpected surprises or effort on my part had to be made. This life habit, life cycle, repeated itself day after day. For years, I thought that this was the only way to survive, and I convinced myself that that's life.

I knew that my **EAT**s were not advantageous to me, but I chose this **EAT** loop simply by not doing anything about it. I was afraid and unwilling to communicate with myself. For what? I didn't think I deserved a better life at the time. It was only after I became aware of my own free will and the real meaning of unconditional self-love that I was able to apply my inner strength/willpower to the investigation of my **E**motions, **A**ctions/behaviors, and **T**houghts and courageously choose a better life for myself.

No matter what you think about your life in this moment, you deserve better.

We **ALL** deserve a better life.

Today, I know that the advice of the professionals whom I frequented was right on: the **answers** to a life of hope, peace, joy, and love truly do come from within.

Now, I have the tools to
    Investigate and
    Discover who I really am,
        and by
    Examining my discoveries, I am able to choose my
        Emotions, Actions/behaviors, and Thoughts, thereby
    Developing myself and my life
        as I choose, consciously.

The essence of knowledge is self-knowledge.
—Plato (428/427—348/347 BC)

Unconsciously, you have chosen to create your individual identity throughout your life; consciousness is the mirror that reflects what you have chosen.

CHAPTER 6

Journaling

The art of writing is the art of
discovering what you believe.
—GUSTAVE FLAUBERT (1821—1880)

Benefits

WHAT ARE THE HEALTH BENEFITS OF JOURNALING?

JOURNALING CREATES AN oasis that can enhance external knowledge and self-knowledge and can promote inner love/self-love. It has been proven to have many benefits, from stretching your IQ and increasing your vocabulary to boosting memory and confidence, evoking mindfulness, and supporting you in the achievement of your goals. Journaling can strengthen and build your self-discipline, self-communication, creativity, and comprehension. Research has also proven that constructive writing, such as journal writing, can be used as a tool for healing the **Body** and **Soul:Minds**. Writing helps to improve the immune system. A daily writing habit has been shown to improve one's ability to manage and organize time. Studies have also shown that the emotional release from **"journaling lowers anxiety, stress, and depression and induces better sleep."**[6]

---

6 Thai Nguyen, "10 Surprising Benefits You'll Get from Keeping a Journal," *Huffington Post*, February 13, 2015, https://www.huffingtonpost.com/thai-nguyen/benefits-of-journaling-_b_6648884.html.

Expressive writing through journaling is a route to healing—emotionally, physically, and psychologically. James Pennebaker, author of *Writing to Heal*, said that he has witnessed improved immune function in participants of writing exercises. Stress often comes from emotional blockages and overthinking hypotheticals.[7] "When we translate an experience into language we essentially make the experience graspable," Pennebaker said. He continues to explain that in doing so, you free yourself from mentally being tangled in traumas.[8]

Journaling daily can release the buildup incurred by your **EAT**s by discovering what it is you want to change/transform in the first place. By becoming aware of, acknowledging, and communicating with yourself, you enable the creation of a safe, loving haven in which to transform your life.

I believe that everything in life happens **for** me and **is** for a reason. I have learned to accept what I possess, all of the so-called *good and bad*, and transform it to suit the life I want and choose to create for myself. When you create a transformation from within, well-established, deep-rooted change is inevitable.

(Note: I prefer to call this process a transformation instead of a change throughout this guide because personally I have learned [through journaling] that when I made changes in the past, the life experience I was trying to change would return to me in some way. For me, a change means forgetting the past and creating something new. A transformation means examining the past and learning from it in order to transform it into what I consciously want to create from the experience. The life experience can never be forgotten or changed; it happened *for* me to learn and develop from and therefore has a reason, a purpose.)

---

7 Ibid.
8 Ibid.; James W. Pennebaker, *Writing to Heal: A Guided Journal for Recovering from Trauma and Emotional Upheaval* (Oakland, CA: New Harbinger, 2004).

Transformation or lasting change is based on the habitual **I**nvestigation, **D**iscovery, **E**xamination, and **D**evelopment of your current **E**motions, **A**ctions/behaviors, and **T**houghts. In doing so, you become more aware of who you are. You become more aware of your beliefs and values, the source of your **EAT**s.

Perception and Quantum Theory

HOW CAN JOURNALING IN *ME: LIFE GUIDE AND GUIDED JOURNEY BY JOURNAL* TRANSFORM THE WAY I PERCEIVE MY REALITY?
Discovering yourself is as simple as observing yourself in this moment—observing your habits, which are readily discoverable through your current **EAT**s. In doing so, you can consciously choose to create and transform perceptions of your past, present, and future.

The self-awareness/self-knowledge gained by journaling on a daily basis can be used as a guide to create, strengthen, transform, and develop patterns of **EAT**s in order to open up new possibilities and shift your direction. This happens simply by observing yourself and observing how you influence—and are influenced—by others and your **Environment** as a whole. Observation, consciousness, and awareness are all linked, and each is an important part of the developmental process by which we reveal knowledge of our perceived reality and then learn from and develop that knowledge to create desirable habits and patterns of **EAT**s. Constructive journaling optimizes this process.

Quantum theory proves this phenomenon. In a research article published by ScienceDaily, the effect is described as follows: "One of the most bizarre premises of quantum theory, which has long fascinated philosophers and physicists alike, states that by the very act of watching, the observer affects the observed reality."[9]

---

9 Weizmann Institute of Science, "Quantum Theory Demonstrated: Observation Affects Reality," *ScienceDaily*, February 27, 1998, https://www.sciencedaily.com/releases/1998/02/980227055013.htm.

Journaling with *Me: Life Guide and Guided Journey by Journal* provides a platform for self-observance and self-communication, therefore consciously affecting, influencing, creating, and transforming your reality. In other words, choosing to create your reality by applying quantum theory to your own life—observing yourself while completing the **7 Soul:Minds Exercises** will indeed affect, influence, transform, and consciously create your reality.

Guided Journaling

HOW DOES THIS GUIDED JOURNEY BY JOURNAL WORK?

Me: Life Guide and Guided Journey by Journal was created for the purpose of discovering who you are and then creating and developing yourself into who you want to be, all the while instilling **EAT**s of love, happiness, and gratitude, which create internal balance and harmony through the practice of the **7 Soul:Minds Exercises** at the end of each day. Through journaling, you can become more aware of and distinguish between conscious and unconscious habits that radiate through your **Body** and surroundings/**Environment**. Expressive journaling can be used to draw attention to specific details of your life, thereby elevating your consciousness/awareness and enabling you to use your free will, your gift to choose, to transform and create the life you want and consciously choose to live.

Discovering who you really are generates awareness of the spectrum of beliefs, values, **E**motions, **A**ctions/behaviors, and **T**houghts that exist within you. Simply by observing them, you can choose to create and practice the **EAT**s that will enable you to live a more harmonious life. This process begins with learning to love who you are in this very moment—without conditions.

Habitual expressive journaling shapes and creates mental "muscles" the same way physical exercise and training regimens shape physical muscles in your body. Muscles are built through exercise routines that challenge your body to break down and rebuild tissue in order to create and define muscles; your brain, nervous system, organs, and so on function in the same manner. By exercising and challenging your **Soul:Minds**, you can consciously create and shape your **E**motions, **A**ctions/behaviors, and **T**houghts, which are easily accessible through practicing self-communication. The saying "Use it or lose it" applies here. Inner strength/willpower, time, patience, repetition, and awareness of your body and your **EAT**s are all important components in developing and strengthening your brain, nervous system, muscles, organs—your entire body—mentally and physically.

Creating, building, transforming and shaping yourself mentally and physically take commitment and time—days, months, even years. We are all unique, we evolve, and each one of us holds our own individual developmental physical and mental timing. This is exactly how you have become who you are today. Consciously, subconsciously, and unconsciously, you have created yourself with your unique developmental time line.

Importance of a Routine before Sleep

WHAT IS THE IMPORTANCE OF EXERCISING MY SOUL:MINDS AT THE END OF EACH DAY?
By now, most of us have pretty much figured out that sleep is a requirement for mental and physical health. Pull an all-nighter and it becomes even more apparent just how much sleep is an important factor in your life. To slumber is a necessity for human beings, but are you aware that the minutes before you fall asleep can make a big difference in how you feel, behave, and think the next day?

In an article titled "Sleep-Dependent Learning and Memory Consolidation," Matthew P. Walker and Robert Stickgold write, "One of the most exciting and contentious hypotheses is that sleep contributes importantly to memory. A large number of studies offer a substantive body of evidence supporting this role of sleep in what is becoming known as sleep-dependent memory processing."[10]

Current Biology published an article stating that "the brain processes complex stimuli during sleep, and uses this information to make decisions while awake."[11] As you sleep, your brain makes decisions, creates and consolidates memories, makes creative connections, clears out toxins, learns, and remembers how to perform tasks, as well as many other things.[12]

Have you ever noticed that at the end of the day, about five to ten minutes before you fall asleep, your **Minds** tend to get busy calculating your **EAT**s and trying to make sense of the happenings of the day—and of your life, for that matter? They do this by applying your perceived knowledge of others and using your own **EAT**s, beliefs, and values in the process of organization and elimination that ultimately forms your conscious, subconscious, and unconscious **Minds (Soul:Minds)**.

Your perceived **EAT**s of the day are compiled and sorted and used for your individual development and growth processes. They are used in creating and transforming your system of beliefs and values and in developing the **E**motions, **A**ctions/behaviors, and **T**houghts that will be uploaded and saved to your **Minds** as you sleep. All of this is accomplished whether you are aware of it or not. Now you can understand further why the **7 Soul:Minds Exercises** are such an important part of your end-of-day—before-sleep—routine.

---

10 Matthew P. Walker and Robert Stickgold, "Sleep-Dependent Learning and Memory Consolidation," *Neuron* 44, no. 1 (2004): 121–133, https://doi.org/10.1016/j.neuron.2004.08.031.
11 Sid Kouider et al., "Inducing Task-Relevant Responses to Speech in the Sleeping Brain," *Current Biology* 24, no. 18 (2014): 2208–2214.
12 Walker and Stickgold, "Sleep-Dependent Learning and Memory Consolidation"; Gregoire, "5 Amazing Things Your Brain Does while You Sleep."

Your **Soul:Minds** store your **E**motions, **A**ctions/behaviors, and **T**houghts and relay who you are to you and to the outside world. Your **Soul:Minds** shape your personality and, among other things, make you unique. They also guide and direct you to where you consciously and unconsciously want to be in your life. You can be sure that wherever you are in your life at this very moment, your conscious, subconscious, and unconscious **E**motions, **A**ctions/behaviors, and **T**houghts have guided you there.

You and only you hold the power to choose how you create your life. The power to choose—free will and willpower—are gifts that we all possess. Yet some of us are not aware of these amazing gifts and seemingly would rather be driven around, taking the back seat in life and remaining unconscious, unaware, and afraid.

Accepting and claiming responsibility for who you have become—who you are—and taking control of your life by steering your **EAT**s in the direction that you consciously choose and want for yourself is life altering. The journey begins with self-communication and becoming aware of the habits of **E**motions, **A**ctions/behaviors, and **T**houghts that have made you who you are today.

Every moment, we are on our individual journey of life. We are able to consciously learn from and choose our destinations by forming positive life habits. This is precisely the outcome of the **7 Soul:Minds Exercises** that make up this guided journal. Doing the exercises at the end of each day for at least 11 weeks will grant you habits that will guide you to the destinations of love, happiness, peace, hope, and gratitude for yourself and your surroundings each day, no matter the circumstances. Furthermore, as you sleep, you will unconsciously reinforce and engrave into the memories of your **Soul:Minds** and the cells that make up your **Body** the **E**motions, **A**ctions, and **T**houghts of love, happiness, peace, hope, and gratitude that will be mapped out for the following day's journey.

You can most definitely transform yourself at your core. By observing and becoming aware of your **EAT**s, you allow for their transformation. In the process, you transform your beliefs and values to those of your choice. Quantum theory proves this—what is observed changes/transforms.

Loving yourself enough to spend the time and effort to investigate and examine who you have become and to discover your **EAT**s, your dreams, and your passions allows for the conscious development of your true self. You will truly be *living* your life as opposed to merely existing.

To live is the rarest thing in the world.
Most people just exist.
—Oscar Wilde (1854—1900)

Live on purpose.

CHAPTER 7

Tools

The Tools

THE BASIS FOR creating, transforming, and supporting a more balanced and harmonious life is to consciously choose the following:

- **Unconditional Self-Love**—choosing to engage in self-compassion and loving yourself for who you are right now, in this moment, without judgment.
- **Healthy Lifestyle**—exercising, eating nutritiously for optimal health, becoming aware of your **EAT**ing habits, quality sleep, meditating, and so on.
- **Creativity/Entertainment**—embracing adventure, hobbies, art, dancing, laughter, amusement, constructive writing, imagination, and so on.
- **Self-Communication/Personal Development**—self-consciousness, self-discovery, self-knowledge, personal growth, and transformation accomplished through journaling, reading books, taking courses, studying, and so on.
- **Self-awareness**—asking, "Have I **ID'ED** my **EAT**s?" Have I **I**nvestigated, **D**iscovered, **E**xamined and **D**eveloped my **E**motions, **A**ctions/behaviors, and **T**houghts with the knowledge that what has happened in the past, what is happening now, and what will happen in the future are all *for* me to learn and develop? Am I aware that my **EAT**s are dynamic and that each one supports, strengthens, and develops the others?

- **Gratitude and Forgiveness**—true forgiveness allows for true gratefulness. Gratitude and forgiveness are connected and complement each other. In order to be truly grateful, we must be able to forgive ourselves and others. Pure gratitude for the lessons received every moment of every day, along with an underlying understanding that life was, is, and will be happening *for* me to learn and develop propels and feeds my ability to forgive; all the while, I'm learning and developing from the people, places, things, and situations that influence my life—*for a reason.* You will know when you are truly grateful for what you have and who you are, because blame, anger, sorrow, judgment, and resentment simply cannot exist in a grateful environment.

Using these tools, I create self-empathy and an overall awareness of who I am.

I have learned and will continue to learn and aspire to love myself just as I am, without self-flagellation and with unconditional love and understanding for the rest of my life.

During my self-investigation, I realized that many of my **E**motions, **A**ctions/behaviors, and **T**houghts stem from memories and patterns acquired in childhood. Today, as an adult, I know that I have the power of my inner strength/free will/willpower, and I can choose the life **I** want to live with love, gratitude, and forgiveness because everything is *for* a reason.

Fear

WHAT ABOUT FEAR?

I believe that the opposite of fear is hope and that they both dwell within me. Fear of the unknown still exists in my life, as it must exist in any process. I meet fear in many different ways—unexpectedly, in new goals, projects, and so on. Fear is a reality for us all. It is an important part of life and can be used as a tool. Fear allows us to hope, to be courageous in order to learn, grow, and develop in our lives. Fear can hold us back and/ or push us forward into the unknown awakening us to self-discover, self-examine, and self-develop.

Melody of Life

I like to call this process the "melody of life," and by using the tools, one can create harmony within the melody. Melodies consist of high tones, low tones, and different rhythms. Some notes are short, and some are long. Today, I know that I am the composer of my melody, and I choose harmony.

Consciously and habitually granting yourself time at the end of each day to review the "happenings of the day" that have occurred *for* you while they are still fresh in your **Soul:Minds** (conscious, subconscious, and un-conscious **Minds**) before they are downloaded, processed, cleaned out, and stored by your brain as you sleep will transform your life. Through self-investigation each day, you can open the lines of self-communication and allow insight into who you really are, what is important to you, where you are headed in your life, and when and how you **EAT** the way you do.

Observe how your **E**motions, **A**ctions/behaviors, and **T**houghts shape your life and trigger your conscious, subconscious, and unconscious **Minds** to seek out the good that comes from everything. Consciousness reinforces and transforms your brain/central nervous system, your senses, and every cell of your **Body** to become aware of the good that surrounds each and every one of us.

The **7 Soul:Minds Exercises** in this journal are a compilation of the ques-tions I ask myself at the end of each day before going to sleep. Forming the habit of self-communication through journaling will support you while answering the question, "Who am I, really?" Ultimately, all the answers that you need and/or you are looking for in life are discoverable from within you.

7 Soul:Minds Exercises Explained

WHAT ARE THE 7 SOUL:MINDS EXERCISES AND HOW WILL THEY INFLUENCE MY LIFE?

Soul:Minds Exercise #1 REVIEW

re·view
(noun)

- a formal assessment or examination of something with the possibility or intention of instituting change if necessary.

TODAY, AFTER REVIEWING MY DAY, WHAT EMOTIONS, ACTIONS/ BEHAVIORS, AND THOUGHTS (EATS) ARISE?

Human beings evolve and grow; it is in our nature. Every moment has a purpose and is there *for* you. The **E**motions, **A**ctions/behaviors, and **T**houghts you feel, act on, and think each moment reflect who you are and give you a glimpse of where you are headed in your life. Each moment can be a beacon, a guiding light to help you discover, examine, and develop yourself. Paying attention to and observing what has happened **for** you during the day will provide you with the information needed to conduct a self-investigation into who you are. Life happens *for* a reason, *for* you.

Finding is reserved for those who search.
—JIM ROHN (1930—2009)

Your life's journey is carefully and precisely mapped out and waiting for you to discover.

Soul:Minds Exercise #2 HAPPINESS

hap·py
(adjective)

- feeling or showing pleasure or contentment.

TODAY, WHAT MADE (AND STILL MAKES) ME HAPPY? DESCRIBE EATs.

There is an old saying that what you look for, you will find. I agree. If you look for happiness, you will find it. If you look for it habitually, you will train yourself to find the good in yourself, people, places, things, events, and so on, and the happier your life will become, even in the worst of circumstances. Being able to discover the good that accompanies every experience in your life is an art and a habit.

The art of being happy lies in the power of extracting happiness from common things.
—HENRY WARD BEECHER (1813—1887)

Soul:Minds Exercise #3 SELF-LOVE

self-love
(noun)

- regard for one's own well-being and happiness (chiefly considered as a desirable rather than narcissistic characteristic).

TODAY, HOW DID I LOVE MYSELF? DESCRIBE EATS.

Self-love is the basis of all love. Every moment of every day brings with it the opportunity to love yourself. Taking the time to eat well, exercise, sleep, create, read, journal, discover, maybe do nothing at all, and learn more about yourself from it all are some of the wonderful ways of loving yourself. Setting aside time and effort to self-investigate at the end of each day is an example of great love for yourself.

Learning to love yourself is the greatest love of all.
—LINDA CREED (1948—1986)

Soul·Minds Exercise #4 BROTHERLY LOVE

broth·er·ly love
(noun)

- feelings* of humanity and compassion toward one's fellow humans.

(*Note: I would add **Actions** and **Thoughts** to complete the **EAT**s.)

TODAY, HOW DID I LOVE OTHERS? DESCRIBE EATS.

Obviously, we are in this world together. Whether we are aware of it or not, the people, animals, nature, things, and others that surround us are there for a purpose. Discovering self-love in exercise #2 allows for the discovery of brotherly love, which is practiced in and with your **Environment**. Your surroundings are an extension of you and exist to influence and teach you about yourself (especially the people, places, things, and events that you do *not* want in your life but are happening *for* you). Loving all aspects of your life can drastically transform your life. In loving, finding the good that comes from your **Environment**/surroundings, you are loving others, things, and nature, and through them, you are essentially loving yourself.

Happiness is in your ability to love others.
When you love someone, you love
the person as they are,
and not as you'd like them to be.
—LEO TOLSTOY (1828—1910)

Soul·Minds Exercise #5 LIFE LESSONS

life les·son
(noun)

- something from which useful knowledge or principles can be learned.

TODAY, WHAT DID I LEARN ABOUT MYSELF? WHAT DID I LEARN IN GENERAL? DESCRIBE THE EATS CREATED FROM THE LESSONS.

Evolving is a part of human nature. Whether you are aware of it or not, you transform, learn, develop, influence, and are influenced through your **Environment**/surroundings every moment. Your brain processes, organizes, and stores information that is relayed to it through your senses. Discovering the good from life lessons and learning about yourself from what has happened *for* you today will advance you in your growth and developmental processes and transform your perspectives; therefore transforming your future for the better.

**The most valuable lessons in life
are not taught but experienced.**

Soul:Minds Exercise #6 GOALS

goal
(noun)

- the object of a person's ambition or effort; an aim or desired result.

WHAT IS/ARE MY GOAL(S) FOR TOMORROW?

**BY ACCOMPLISHING MY GOAL(S) WHAT WILL IT/THEY ALLOW ME TO
ACHIEVE, AND HOW WILL MY GOAL(S) INFLUENCE MY EATS?**
DID I ACCOMPLISH THE GOAL(S) I SET FOR MYSELF YESTERDAY?
(YES/NO)
IF NOT, WHAT STEPS WILL I TAKE TO ACCOMPLISH THEM?

Having goals in life keeps us *alive*. You can live without goals, but to truly be *alive*, it's imperative to set goals and then aim and aspire to make them your reality. In writing your goals down, you are activating your brain and sparking your neurons to organize and construct **EAT**s that will support you in achieving them. When you set goals with the intention of accomplishing them, your brain and nervous system will automatically get to work on how to produce, perform, and make them happen as you sleep. Setting goals is the prerequisite to taking action and following through on your ideas, dreams, and your passions in life.

We all have goals, dreams, and a purpose. That is why we are here in the first place, whether we know what our goals, dreams, and purposes are or not. Your purpose may be to become one or more of the following: a family member, a friend, a businessperson, a writer, an artist, a swimmer, a gardener, a recycler, a politician, a surfer, a captain, a seamstress, a designer, a lawyer, a scientist, a therapist, a traveler, and so on. You name it. We all have goals in life (even if we are unaware of them). They are there for us to learn, improve on, and live our passions. What are you passionate about? What can you do tomorrow to grow and develop that passion? Live your purpose. This is your chance, your time to shine because you are here to do just that; no matter what age you happen to be in this moment.

Tip: To assist yourself in accomplishing your goals for the following day, it is helpful to write them in your daily planner or on a recycled sheet of paper to be used as a reference the next day—a reminder of the goal(s) you have set for yourself.

If you want to live a happy life, tie it to a goal,
not to people or objects.
—Albert Einstein (1879—1955)

Soul:Minds Exercise #7 GRATITUDE

grat·i·tude
(noun)

- the quality of being thankful; readiness to show appreciation for and to return kindness.

TODAY, FOR WHOM AND FOR WHAT AM I GRATEFUL? DESCRIBE THE REASONS. DESCRIBE EATS.

I believe that this is the MOST IMPORTANT EXERCISE. If, at the end of your day, you find that you have absolutely *no* energy to exercise your **Soul:Minds**, please find the strength to complete this exercise.

Gratitude supports life. Being grateful for the opportunities in and of life will give you a more optimistic outlook in and about your own life. This is a prosperous way to conclude your day. Recognizing and distinguishing at least two gratifiers from your day a person and a place, thing, and/or event will advance your life development process. Two big self-gratifiers that come to mind at the moment are the ability to breathe and the fact that you are alive. **Life is a gift**—and an **extraordinary** one at that. Reward yourself with this gift every day by discovering *all* that there is to be grateful for in your life.

Feeling gratitude and not expressing it
is like wrapping a present and not giving it.
—WILLIAM ARTHUR WARD (1921—1994)

For more information, here are two scientific references on the importance of gratitude:

- R. A. Emmons and M. E. McCullough, "Counting Blessings versus Burdens: An Experimental Investigation of Gratitude and Subjective Well-Being in Daily Life," *Journal of Personal Social Pschology* 84, no. 2 (2003): 377–389, https://www.ncbi.nlm.nih.gov/pubmed/12585811.
- Alex Korb, "The Grateful Brain: The Neuroscience of Giving Thanks," *Psychology Today*, November 20, 2012, https://www.psychologytoday.com/blog/prefrontal-nudity/201211/the-grateful-brain.

If you are curious to know how I feel about my life and childhood today, I wouldn't want it any other way. I am **me** because of every person, place, thing, and event that has influenced, influences, and will influence my life. Journaling has supported me to become more aware of and deeply grateful for all of my life lessons. I am truly grateful for my past, present and **all** of the people, places, things, and events that have supported me in the creation of the one and only *me*.

Life always happens *for* a reason, especially *for* you.

There is a reason for each and every one of us. You are truly special, and you matter.

Tending to all aspects of your life as you would a cherished garden—by observing and feeding your **Spirit~Soul:Minds~Body~Environment** with kindness, compassion, love, and gratitude—will support you in reaping the same for your life as you grow and develop every moment of every day.

You are worth it. Start living the life you deserve by discovering who you are while completing the **7 Soul:Minds Exercises**, creating and developing **EAT**s that you consciously want in your life, even while you sleep.

I hope and wish for you an enlightened, wonderful journey surrounded and enveloped by unconditional self-love as you investigate the most important question you could ever ask yourself in life—"Who am I, really?"—and receive your answers from within.

With unconditional love....Jennifer ☺

Frequently Asked Questions

ARE THERE ANY INSTRUCTIONS TO FOLLOW WHILE JOURNALING IN
ME: LIFE GUIDE AND GUIDED JOURNEY BY JOURNAL?
At the end of each day, before you begin to journey by journal and completing the **7 Soul:Minds Exercises**, you may find it helpful to close your eyes and take a few slow, deep breaths. Closing the eyelids heightens all other senses and allows you to become more self-aware. By breathing deeply and rhythmically, you gain access to a clearer mind and stronger focusing abilities. You may do so by inhaling slowly, filling your lungs and midriff area with air to the count of seven, holding your breath to a count of three, and then exhaling to a count of seven. Repeat this at least three times. After you have completed the breathing exercises, with your eyes still closed, observe and review your day, from the moment you woke up to the very moment before you begin to write in your journal, using your **Soul:Minds'** eye, your **EAT**s, as the basis in answering the **7 Soul:Minds Exercises.**

Remembering that everyone, every place, everything, every event/situation you encountered today was and is *for* a reason, simply allow yourself to observe without judgment and/or criticism of yourself or others. When you are ready, open your eyes feeling more relaxed, focused, and ready to complete the **7 Soul:Minds Exercises**.

If you would like to expand on one or more of the **Soul:Minds Exercises**, feel free to do so on a separate sheet of recycled paper.

WHAT IF I DON'T FEEL COMFORTABLE WRITING DOWN MY INNERMOST
EATS ON PAPER? IS THERE ANOTHER WAY?
Writing down and documenting who you are is exposing yourself, and for good reason. To be able to choose the life you want to live, you need to become aware of and be content and in harmony with who you are right

now. Your documented **EAT**s serve as a reference and support you in your developmental process.

While I definitely recommend storing your journal pages as a reference, in order to ease your **Minds**, you most definitely can choose to relinquish them in any way you see fit. It is better to have exercised your **Soul:Minds** and had the chance to become aware of them, than never to have exercised your **Soul:Minds** at all.

Why is this guided-journal process 11 weeks long?

Me: Life Guide and Guided Journey by Journal is based on a set of questions that when asked and answered at the end of each day for the duration of 11 weeks, form more positive life habits. 11 weeks is a sufficient amount of time to form a habit according to research.[13]

What should I do if I miss a day or two, or more?

Creating new habits will take inner strength, willpower, patience, and persistence. Journaling at the end of each day may seem overwhelming at first and may become challenging even for the most dedicated journaler. Some days, you may not feel like writing. You may encounter feelings of exhaustion, frustration, and so on. These are all part of any new formed habit. I, too, could give in to my exhaustion on any given day during the 11 week period. I realize there may be some obstacles. Life is full of challenges, but they make it that much more exciting and spark your willpower to come *alive* instead of merely existing.

Sometimes habits are not as easy to form as you think. Please do not to give up. Keep up the sequence, day-by-day, as much as possible. Be aware of your obstacles. Overcoming them will be well worth your effort. If it makes you feel, act, or think any better, researchers have discovered that "it doesn't matter if you mess up every now and then. Building better

---

13 Clear, "How Long Does It Actually Take to Form a New Habit? (Backed by Science)."

habits is not an all-or-nothing process."[14] If you find that you have absolutely no energy to exercise your **Soul:Minds** at the end of your day please give brief answers or just complete **Soul:Minds Exercise #7: Gratitude**.

If you discover that you haven't exercised your **Soul:Minds** on consecutive days, forgive yourself. It is part of the process. Write about it and then pick up where you left off, all the while loving yourself unconditionally. The intention of this guided journal is to maintain continuity with flexibility, which allows for true self-expression through communication.

WHAT SHOULD I EXPECT TO HAPPEN DURING THE 11 WEEKS?

All information gained by observing and becoming aware of yourself and your **Environment**/surroundings will support you in your life's journey, discovery, examination, and development to create the life you want to live. Communication is a skill we learn in order to interact with others and express ourselves. The desired outcome or goals of any communication process are awareness, consciousness, and an overall understanding of ourselves and others.

Forming new habits takes practice, and it comes with its own challenges. Answering the question, "Who am I, really?" is not an overnight, a weekly, or even yearly task. It is a question we will ask ourselves throughout our lives. Choosing to search for the answers to who we really are through self-communication enables us to discover them in a more advanced, peaceful, and loving way.

At first, you may encounter resistance. You may be too tired. You may not want to do the exercises. You may doubt their utility. Many **EAT**s ran through my head when I began to complete the **7 Soul:Minds Exercises**. Please flex your inner strength/willpower and stick with it; you will discover, create, and develop habits that will transform you into the person you choose and want to be. What you practice you will perfect.

---

14 Pennebaker, *Writing to Heal.*

WHAT HAPPENS AFTER I HAVE COMPLETED 11 WEEKS OF JOURNALING?

When you have completed 11 weeks of the guided journal portion of *Me: Life Guide and Guided Journey by Journal* and as you continue on your life's journey, you may choose to extend and maintain the exercising of your **Soul:Minds** in this same manner. Journaling has become a constructive habit of mine and an end-of-the-day routine that I will probably continue for the rest of my life. The exercises keep me focused, aware, and on track. They support me in setting and accomplishing goals. Choosing to continue to self-communicate through journaling will further self-support and strengthen your awareness and communication skills.

After completing 11 weeks of guided journaling and becoming more aware of who you are, please do not stop questioning yourself. Always look forward to the answers you will receive from within. Life is a journey. Allow your **EAT**s to be your compass. They will guide you to better understand and develop who you really are and who you were born to be because life happens *for* a reason, on purpose.

For support, additional information, and/or comments, please contact www.hometopurpose.com.

References

Bianconi, E. et al. "An Estimation of the Number of Cells in the Human Body." *Annals of Human Biology* 40, no. 6 (2013): 463–471. https://doi: 10.3109/03014460.2013.807878.

Clear, James. "How Long Does It Actually Take to Form a New Habit? (Backed by Science)." *Huffington Post*, June 10, 2014. https://www.huffingtonpost.com/james-clear/forming-new-habits_b_5104807.html.

Duhigg, Charles. *The Power of Habit: Why We Do What We Do in Life and Business.* New York: Random House, 2014.

Emmons, Robert A., and Michael E. McCullough. "Counting Blessings versus Burdens: An Experimental Investigation of Gratitude and Subjective Well-Being in Daily Life." *Journal of Personality and Social Psychology* 84, no. 2 (2003): 377–389. http://psycnet.apa.org/record/2003-01140-012?doi=1.

"Gravity." *Wikipedia.* Retrieved January 6, 2018. https://en.wikipedia.org/wiki/Gravity.

Gregoire, Carolyn. "5 Amazing Things Your Brain Does while You Sleep." *Huffington Post*, September 29, 2014. https://www.huffingtonpost.com/2014/09/28/brain-sleep-_n_5863736.html.

Hewings-Martin, Yella. "How Many Cells Are in the Human Body." *Medical News Today*, July 12, 2017. https://www.medicalnewstoday.com/articles/318342.php.

"How Does the Nervous System Work? Informed Health Online." *NCBI PubMed Health*, August 19, 2016. https://www.ncbi.nlm.nih.gov/pubmedhealth/PMH0072574/.

Korb, Alex. "The Grateful Brain: The Neuroscience of Giving Thanks." *Psychology Today*, November 20, 2012. https://www.psychologytoday.com/blog/prefrontal-nudity/201211/the-grateful-brain.

Lally, Phillippa et al. "How Are Habits Formed? Modeling Habit Formation in the Real World." *European Journal of Social Psychology* 40, no. 6 (2010): 998–1009. https://doi.org/:10.1002/ejsp.674.

Nguyen, Thai. "10 Surprising Benefits You'll Get from Keeping a Journal." *Huffington Post*, December 6, 2017. https://www.huffingtonpost.com/thai-nguyen/benefits-of-journaling-_b_6648884.html.

Pennebaker, James W. *Writing to Heal: A Guided Journal for Recovering from Trauma and Emotional Upheaval.* Oakland, CA: New Harbinger, 2004.

Sid Kouider, Thomas Andrillon, Leonardo S. Barbosa, Louise Goupil, and Tristan A. Bekinschtein. "Inducing Task-Relevant Responses to Speech in the Sleeping Brain." *Current Biology* 24, no. 18. (2014): 2208–2214. http://www.cell.com/current-biology/fulltext/S0960-9822(14)00994-4.

Walker, Matthew P., and Robert Stickgold. "Sleep-Dependent Learning and Memory Consolidation." *Neuron* 44, no. 1 (2004): 121–133. https://doi.org/10.1016/j.neuron.2004.08.031.

Weizmann Institute of Science. "Quantum Theory Demonstrated: Observation Affects Reality." *ScienceDaily*, February 27, 1998. https://www.sciencedaily.com/releases/1998/02/980227055013.htm.

PART 2

Guided Journey by Journal

Featuring 11 Weeks of 7 Soul:Minds Exercises

Emotions List

WHAT IS THE EMOTIONS LIST, AND WHAT IS ITS PURPOSE?

WE ALL POSSESS every emotion from sad to glad, frustrated to elated, jealous to content, and so on. Emotions are energy in motion and like batteries; they are the power source of your life energy. Your chosen perspective of your positive (+) emotions and negative (–) emotions charge your power source feeding your life energy. Both positive and negative emotions are needed for a charge; becoming aware of all of your emotions will allow you to consciously choose how you act and think about your life and who you are.

On the following page, you will discover a condensed list of emotions that will guide you to the more precise emotions you are feeling and/ or have felt throughout the day. If you are feeling an emotion that is not listed, please feel free to add it. Use any and all descriptions of your emotions. Doing so will enhance your personal awareness and support you on your guided journey.

The emotions list is included as a reference to support and assist the expansion of emotional awareness. It may be detached and used as a page marker within *Me: Life Guide and Guided Journey by Journal* for quick access and daily use. Remember: At the end of the day, it is you who chooses how you will **EAT** (**E**motion, **A**ct, and **T**hink).

Genius is the ability to renew one's
emotions in daily experience.
—PAUL CÉZANNE (1839—1906)

Happy	Ecstatic	Calm	Grateful	Love
amused	blissful	balanced	appreciative	admired
cheerful	elated	centered	blessed	accepting
delighted	enthralled	clear headed	charmed	affectionate
glad	enthusiastic	comfortable	fortunate	attentive
great	euphoria	content	gifted	attracted
joyful	exhilarated	equanimous	lucky	caring
jubilant	exuberant	fulfilled	moved	compassionate
pampered	overjoyed	harmonious	thankful	considerate
pleased	radiant	low-key	thoughtful	devoted
sunny	rapturous	mellow	touched	empathetic
tickled	thrilled	neutral		faithful
		peaceful	**Interested**	friendly
Excited	**Confident**	placid	absorbed	generous
amazed	assured	quiet	alert	loyal
ardent	courageous	relaxed	curious	kindness
aroused	determined	relieved	enchanted	nonjudgmental
astonished	empowered	resolved	engaged	openhearted
dazzled	open	satisfied	engrossed	open-minded
eager	positive	serene	entranced	passionate
energetic	proud	still	fascinated	respected
enthusiastic	sage	tranquil	intrigued	sensitive
giddy	secure	trusting	involved	sympathetic
invigorated	self-sufficient		spellbound	tender
joyous		**Renewed**	stimulated	trust
lively	**Optimistic**	dynamic		valued
passionate	cheerful	enlivened	**Strong**	warm
surprised	encouraged	improved	able	
vibrant	expectant	peaceful	certain	**Alive**
	hopeful	reborn	daring	energetic
Patient	hoping	recovered	dynamic	free
at ease	idealistic	refreshed	hardy	frisky
at peace	inspired	rejuvenated	intent	impulsive
bright	kind	repaired	keen	liberated
content	respected	rested	sure	playful
pleased	wonder	restored	tenacious	spirited
reassured	worthy	revived	unique	wonderful

Sad	Hate	Confused	Hurt	Helpless
depressed	animosity	ambivalent	agony	alone
despair	appalled	baffled	anguished	clingy
despondent	contempt	bewildered	bereaved	dominated
disappointed	disgusted	concerned	bullied	fragile
discouraged	dislike	conflicted	defeated	guarded
disheartened	horrified	dazed	devastated	indecisive
forlorn	hostile	doubtful	heartbroken	insecure
gloomy	inferior	flustered	isolated	leery
heavyhearted	repulsed	hesitant	lonely	powerless
hopeless		lost	miserable	reserved
melancholy	**Annoyed**	mystified	regretful	sensitive
tearful	aggravated	perplexed	remorseful	shaky
unhappy	disgruntled	puzzled	sorrow	vulnerable
wretched	dismayed	shy	tormented	
	displeased	stuck	threatened	**Rejected**
Afraid	exasperated	torn		alienated
apprehensive	frustrated	uncertain	**Judgmental**	aloof
fearful	impatient		competitive	apathetic
frightened	irritated	**Restless**	defensive	bored
mistrustful	provoked	agitated	insulted	closed-minded
panicked		alarmed	jealous	disconnected
petrified	**Nervous**	disconcerted	longing	distant
scared	anxious	disturbed	nostalgic	distracted
suspicious	anticipate	offended	pining	distrusted
terrified	cranky	perturbed	skeptical	numb
wary	distraught	rattled	wistful	pathetic
worried	distressed	shocked	yearning	removed
	edgy	startled		uninterested
Tired	fidgety	surprised	**Angry**	withdrawn
burnt out	frazzled	troubled	enraged	
depleted	irritable	turmoil	furious	**Embarrassed**
exhausted	jittery	unbelieving	incensed	ashamed
fatigued	overwhelmed	uncomfortable	indignant	chagrined
lazy	restless	uneasy	irate	guilty
lethargic	stressed out	unnerved	livid	humbled
weary	tense	unsettled	outraged	mortified
worn out	unstable	upset	resentful	self-conscious

Weekly Summaries

WHAT ARE "THIS WEEK'S MELODY" AND THE "GOAL SETTER"?

At the end of each week, you will discover "This Week's Melody" and the "Goal Setter." They are weekly awareness summaries and guides. They strengthen skill sets and form new ones for self-awareness, self-discovery, self-examination, and self-development.

It is extremely important to remember that the questions, summaries, and guides are all created for awareness purposes only and should be used without judgment or criticism. Applying unconditional self-love will foster and advance your personal growth and development processes.

"I Do Declare" Affirmation

WHAT IS THE "I DO DECLARE" AFFIRMATION?

The "I Do Declare" affirmation agreement is located on the following page. It is a written declaration of your promise to yourself. After you have read the agreement and filled in the blanks, please re-read it aloud and then sign the agreement that you have made with yourself. Committing to yourself is the first step in the discovery of who you are.

You always have two choices: your
commitment versus your fear.
—SAMMY DAVIS JR. (1925—1990)

I Do Declare

I, _____, understand that I am going on an intensive, guided journey to experience self-awareness and unconditional self-love that will lead me to my true, unique self, my authentic self.

I agree and commit, to the best of my ability, to 11 weeks of self-investigation that will allow me to discover, examine, and develop/create myself. Fatigue, lack of energy, or any other circumstance under my control will not prevent me from discovering and creating my true, unique self.

I hereby release and liberate myself from all past comments, promises, judgments, oaths, vows, and any other self-flagellation that I have undergone consciously, subconsciously, and/or unconsciously that does not further my purpose and promote my goal of loving myself unconditionally.

With unconditional love,

——————————————————————
(Signature)

——————————————————————
(Date)

Please read your "I Do Declare" affirmation **aloud.**

7 Soul:Minds Exercises ~ 11 Weeks

**The most important journey you will embark on in your life
is the journey within.**

Your Journey by Journal Begins...

Me

Date_____Time_____

Tip: With your eyes closed, take a few slow, deep inhalations and exhalations. Review your day, open your eyes, and begin.

1. **Today**, after reviewing my day, what **E**motions, **A**ctions/behaviors, and **T**houghts (**EAT**s) arise?

2. **Today**, what made (and still makes) me happy? Describe **EAT**s.

3. **Today**, how did I love myself? Describe **EAT**s.

4. **Today**, how did I love others? Describe **EAT**s.

5. **Today**, what did I learn about myself? What did I learn in general? Describe the **EAT**s created from the lessons.

6. What is/are my goal(s) for tomorrow? By accomplishing my goal(s), what will it/they allow me to achieve? How will my goal(s) influence my **EAT**s?

7. **Today**, for whom and for what am I grateful? Describe the reasons. Describe **EAT**s.

Learn from yesterday, live for today, hope for tomorrow. The important thing is not to stop questioning.
—Albert Einstein

Date_____**Time**_____

Tip: With your eyes closed, take a few slow, deep inhalations and exhalations. Review your day, open your eyes, and begin.

1. **Today**, after reviewing my day, what **E**motions, **A**ctions/behaviors, and **T**houghts (**EAT**s) arise?

2. **Today**, what made (and still makes) me happy? Describe **EAT**s.

3. **Today**, how did I love myself? Describe **EAT**s.

4. **Today**, how did I love others? Describe **EAT**s.

5. **Today**, what did I learn about myself? What did I learn in general? Describe the **EAT**s created from the lessons.

6. **Today**, did I accomplish the goal(s) I set for myself yesterday? (Yes/No) If not, what steps will I take to accomplish them?
What is/are my goal(s) for tomorrow?
By accomplishing my goal(s), what will it/they allow me to achieve?
How will my goal(s) influence my **EAT**s?

7. **Today**, for whom and for what am I grateful? Describe the reasons. Describe **EAT**s.

If you change the way you look at things,
the things you look at change.
—WAYNE DYER

Me

Date_____Time_____

Tip: With your eyes closed, take a few slow, deep inhalations and exhalations.
Review your day, open your eyes, and begin.

1. **Today**, after reviewing my day, what **E**motions, **A**ctions/behaviors, and **T**houghts (**EAT**s) arise?

2. **Today**, what made (and still makes) me happy? Describe **EAT**s.

3. **Today**, how did I love myself? Describe **EAT**s.

4. **Today**, how did I love others? Describe **EAT**s.

5. **Today**, what did I learn about myself? What did I learn in general? Describe the **EAT**s created from the lessons.

6. **Today**, did I accomplish the goal(s) I set for myself yesterday? (Yes/No) If not, what steps will I take to accomplish them?
What is/are my goal(s) for tomorrow?
By accomplishing my goal(s), what will it/they allow me to achieve?
How will my goal(s) influence my **EAT**s?

7. **Today**, for whom and for what am I grateful? Describe the reasons. Describe **EAT**s.

Life is a succession of lessons which
must be lived to be understood.
—HELEN KELLER

Me

Date_____Time_____

Tip: With your eyes closed, take a few slow, deep inhalations and exhalations. Review your day, open your eyes, and begin.

1. **Today**, after reviewing my day, what **E**motions, **A**ctions/behaviors, and **T**houghts (**EAT**s) arise?

2. **Today**, what made (and still makes) me happy? Describe **EAT**s.

3. **Today**, how did I love myself? Describe **EAT**s.

4. **Today**, how did I love others? Describe **EAT**s.

5. **Today**, what did I learn about myself? What did I learn in general? Describe the **EAT**s created from the lessons.

6. **Today**, did I accomplish the goal(s) I set for myself yesterday? (Yes/No) If not, what steps will I take to accomplish them?
What is/are my goal(s) for tomorrow?
By accomplishing my goal(s), what will it/they allow me to achieve? How will my goal(s) influence my **EAT**s?

7. **Today**, for whom and for what am I grateful? Describe the reasons. Describe **EAT**s.

The only thing we have to fear is fear itself.
—Franklin Delano Roosevelt

Date_____**Time**_____

Tip: With your eyes closed, take a few slow, deep inhalations and exhalations.
Review your day, open your eyes, and begin.

1. **Today**, after reviewing my day, what **E**motions, **A**ctions/behaviors, and **T**houghts (**EAT**s) arise?

2. **Today**, what made (and still makes) me happy? Describe **EAT**s.

3. **Today**, how did I love myself? Describe **EAT**s.

4. **Today**, how did I love others? Describe **EAT**s.

5. **Today**, what did I learn about myself? What did I learn in general? Describe the **EAT**s created from the lessons.

6. **Today**, did I accomplish the goal(s) I set for myself yesterday? (Yes/No) If not, what steps will I take to accomplish them?
   What is/are my goal(s) for tomorrow?
   By accomplishing my goal(s), what will it/they allow me to achieve?
   How will my goal(s) influence my **EAT**s?

7. **Today**, for whom and for what am I grateful? Describe the reasons. Describe **EAT**s.

Most folks are as happy as they
make up their minds to be.
—ABRAHAM LINCOLN

Date_____Time_____

Tip: With your eyes closed, take a few slow, deep inhalations and exhalations.
Review your day, open your eyes, and begin.

1. Today, after reviewing my day, what **E**motions, **A**ctions/behaviors, and **T**houghts (**EAT**s) arise?

2. Today, what made (and still makes) me happy? Describe **EAT**s.

3. Today, how did I love myself? Describe **EAT**s.

4. Today, how did I love others? Describe **EAT**s.

5. **Today**, what did I learn about myself? What did I learn in general? Describe the **EAT**s created from the lessons.

6. **Today**, did I accomplish the goal(s) I set for myself yesterday? (Yes/No) If not, what steps will I take to accomplish them?
   What is/are my goal(s) for tomorrow?
   By accomplishing my goal(s), what will it/they allow me to achieve?
   How will my goal(s) influence my **EAT**s?

7. **Today**, for whom and for what am I grateful? Describe the reasons. Describe **EAT**s.

He who falls in love with himself will have no rivals.
—BENJAMIN FRANKLIN

Me

Date_____Time_____

Tip: With your eyes closed, take a few slow, deep inhalations and exhalations. Review your day, open your eyes, and begin.

1. **Today**, after reviewing my day, what **E**motions, **A**ctions/behaviors, and **T**houghts (**EAT**s) arise?

2. **Today**, what made (and still makes) me happy? Describe **EAT**s.

3. **Today**, how did I love myself? Describe **EAT**s.

4. **Today**, how did I love others? Describe **EAT**s.

5. **Today**, what did I learn about myself? What did I learn in general? Describe the **EAT**s created from the lessons.

6. **Today**, did I accomplish the goal(s) I set for myself yesterday? (Yes/No) If not, what steps will I take to accomplish them?
   What is/are my goal(s) for tomorrow?
   By accomplishing my goal(s), what will it/they allow me to achieve?
   How will my goal(s) influence my **EAT**s?

7. **Today**, for whom and for what am I grateful? Describe the reasons. Describe **EAT**s.

If we all did the things we were capable
of, we would astound ourselves.
—THOMAS EDISON

This Week's Melody

To further your self-discovery and self-awareness this week place music notes (♩) or dots on the music lines below. Each music note/dot will represent the tone/sound you chose to create in the following subjects this week:

♩The top position of the music note/dot on the music lines below represents a high level of fulfillment.

♩The middle position of the music note/dot on the music lines below represents a partial level of fulfillment.

♩The bottom position of the music note/dot on the music lines below represents a desire for further fulfillment.

Gratitude and Forgiveness	Health	Self-Investigation	Creativity/ Entertainment	Relationships	Work/ Education

Gratitude and Forgiveness: Level of thankfulness and forgiveness this week—gratitude and forgiveness for myself and others, using the events that happened *for* me this week.

Health: Level of body nourishment this week—healthy lifestyle, exercise, nutrition, meditation, quality of sleep, and so on.

Self-Investigation: Level of self-awareness this week—discovery, examination, and personal development through reading and writing, expansion of personal knowledge, self-communication, and so on.

Creativity/Entertainment: Level of adventure, enjoyment of hobbies, art, laughter, amusement, and so on this week.

Relationships: Level of communication this week—with family, friends, my community, and so on.

Work/Education: Level of investment in work, career, homemaking (management of the household), and education this week.

Goal Setter	My goal(s) for next week are... Describe EATs.	What step(s) will I take next week to achieve my goal(s)?
Gratitude and Forgiveness		
Health		
Self-Investigation		
Creativity/ Entertainment		
Relationships		
Work/ Education		

Life is a melody, and you are the composer.

Me

Date_____**Time**_____

Tip: With your eyes closed, take a few slow, deep inhalations and exhalations.
Review your day, open your eyes, and begin.

1. **Today**, after reviewing my day, what **E**motions, **A**ctions/behaviors, and **T**houghts (**EAT**s) arise?

2. **Today**, what made (and still makes) me happy? Describe **EAT**s.

3. **Today**, how did I love myself? Describe **EAT**s.

4. **Today**, how did I love others? Describe **EAT**s.

5. **Today**, what did I learn about myself? What did I learn in general? Describe the **EAT**s created from the lessons.

6. **Today**, did I accomplish the goal(s) I set for myself yesterday? (Yes/No) If not, what steps will I take to accomplish them? What is/are my goal(s) for tomorrow? By accomplishing my goal(s), what will it/they allow me to achieve? How will my goal(s) influence my **EAT**s?

7. **Today**, for whom and for what am I grateful? Describe the reasons. Describe **EAT**s.

You must become the producer, director and actor in the unfolding story of your life.
—WAYNE DYER

Date_____Time_____

Tip: With your eyes closed, take a few slow, deep inhalations and exhalations. Review your day, open your eyes, and begin.

1. **Today**, after reviewing my day, what **E**motions, **A**ctions/behaviors, and **T**houghts (**EAT**s) arise?

2. **Today**, what made (and still makes) me happy? Describe **EAT**s.

3. **Today**, how did I love myself? Describe **EAT**s.

4. **Today**, how did I love others? Describe **EAT**s.

5. **Today**, what did I learn about myself? What did I learn in general? Describe the **EAT**s created from the lessons.

6. **Today**, did I accomplish the goal(s) I set for myself yesterday? (Yes/No) If not, what steps will I take to accomplish them? What is/are my goal(s) for tomorrow? By accomplishing my goal(s), what will it/they allow me to achieve? How will my goal(s) influence my **EAT**s?

7. **Today**, for whom and for what am I grateful? Describe the reasons. Describe **EAT**s.

When we seek to discover the best in others, we somehow bring out the best in ourselves.
—WILLIAM ARTHUR WARD

Me

Date_____**Time**_____

Tip: With your eyes closed, take a few slow, deep inhalations and exhalations. Review your day, open your eyes, and begin.

1. **Today**, after reviewing my day, what **E**motions, **A**ctions/behaviors, and **T**houghts (**EAT**s) arise?

2. **Today**, what made (and still makes) me happy? Describe **EAT**s.

3. **Today**, how did I love myself? Describe **EAT**s.

4. **Today**, how did I love others? Describe **EAT**s.

5. **Today**, what did I learn about myself? What did I learn in general? Describe the **EAT**s created from the lessons.

6. **Today**, did I accomplish the goal(s) I set for myself yesterday? (Yes/No) If not, what steps will I take to accomplish them?
What is/are my goal(s) for tomorrow?
By accomplishing my goal(s), what will it/they allow me to achieve?
How will my goal(s) influence my **EAT**s?

7. **Today**, for whom and for what am I grateful? Describe the reasons. Describe **EAT**s.

The man who moves a mountain begins
by carrying away small stones.
—CONFUCIUS

Date_____Time_____

Tip: With your eyes closed, take a few slow, deep inhalations and exhalations.
Review your day, open your eyes, and begin.

1. **Today**, after reviewing my day, what **E**motions, **A**ctions/behaviors, and **T**houghts (**EAT**s) arise?

2. **Today**, what made (and still makes) me happy? Describe **EAT**s.

3. **Today**, how did I love myself? Describe **EAT**s.

4. **Today**, how did I love others? Describe **EAT**s.

5. **Today**, what did I learn about myself? What did I learn in general? Describe the **EAT**s created from the lessons.

6. **Today**, did I accomplish the goal(s) I set for myself yesterday? (Yes/No) If not, what steps will I take to accomplish them?
What is/are my goal(s) for tomorrow?
By accomplishing my goal(s), what will it/they allow me to achieve?
How will my goal(s) influence my **EAT**s?

7. **Today**, for whom and for what am I grateful? Describe the reasons. Describe **EAT**s.

If you always do what you've always done, you
always get what you've always gotten.
—Anonymous

Date_____Time_____

Tip: With your eyes closed, take a few slow, deep inhalations and exhalations.
Review your day, open your eyes, and begin.

1. **Today**, after reviewing my day, what **E**motions, **A**ctions/behaviors, and **T**houghts (**EAT**s) arise?

2. **Today**, what made (and still makes) me happy? Describe **EAT**s.

3. **Today**, how did I love myself? Describe **EAT**s.

4. **Today**, how did I love others? Describe **EAT**s.

5. **Today**, what did I learn about myself? What did I learn in general? Describe the **EAT**s created from the lessons.

6. **Today**, did I accomplish the goal(s) I set for myself yesterday? (Yes/No) If not, what steps will I take to accomplish them?
   What is/are my goal(s) for tomorrow?
   By accomplishing my goal(s), what will it/they allow me to achieve?
   How will my goal(s) influence my **EAT**s?

7. **Today**, for whom and for what am I grateful? Describe the reasons. Describe **EAT**s.

You need to claim the events of your
life to make yourself yours.
—ANNE-WILSON SCHAEF

Me

Date_____Time_____

Tip: With your eyes closed, take a few slow, deep inhalations and exhalations. Review your day, open your eyes, and begin.

1. **Today**, after reviewing my day, what **E**motions, **A**ctions/behaviors, and **T**houghts (**EAT**s) arise?

2. **Today**, what made (and still makes) me happy? Describe **EAT**s.

3. **Today**, how did I love myself? Describe **EAT**s.

4. **Today**, how did I love others? Describe **EAT**s.

5. **Today**, what did I learn about myself? What did I learn in general? Describe the **EAT**s created from the lessons.

6. **Today**, did I accomplish the goal(s) I set for myself yesterday? (Yes/No) If not, what steps will I take to accomplish them?
What is/are my goal(s) for tomorrow?
By accomplishing my goal(s), what will it/they allow me to achieve?
How will my goal(s) influence my **EAT**s?

7. **Today**, for whom and for what am I grateful? Describe the reasons. Describe **EAT**s.

Just remember, you can't climb the ladder of
success with your hands in your pockets.
—ARNOLD SCHWARZENEGGER

Date_____Time_____

Tip: With your eyes closed, take a few slow, deep inhalations and exhalations. Review your day, open your eyes, and begin.

1. **Today**, after reviewing my day, what **E**motions, **A**ctions/behaviors, and **T**houghts (**EAT**s) arise?

2. **Today**, what made (and still makes) me happy? Describe **EAT**s.

3. **Today**, how did I love myself? Describe **EAT**s.

4. **Today**, how did I love others? Describe **EAT**s.

5. **Today**, what did I learn about myself? What did I learn in general? Describe the **EAT**s created from the lessons.

6. **Today**, did I accomplish the goal(s) I set for myself yesterday? (Yes/No) If not, what steps will I take to accomplish them?
What is/are my goal(s) for tomorrow?
By accomplishing my goal(s), what will it/they allow me to achieve?
How will my goal(s) influence my **EAT**s?

7. **Today**, for whom and for what am I grateful? Describe the reasons. Describe **EAT**s.

The journey of a thousand miles begins with one step.
—Lao Tzu

Me

This Week's Melody

To further your self-discovery and self-awareness this week place music notes (♩) or dots on the music lines below. Each music note/dot will represent the tone/sound you chose to create in the following subjects this week:

♩The top position of the music note/dot on the music lines below represents a high level of fulfillment.

♩The middle position of the music note/dot on the music lines below represents a partial level of fulfillment.

♩The bottom position of the music note/dot on the music lines below represents a desire for further fulfillment.

Gratitude and Forgiveness: Level of thankfulness and forgiveness this week—gratitude and forgiveness for myself and others, using the events that happened *for* me this week.

Health: Level of body nourishment this week—healthy lifestyle, exercise, nutrition, meditation, quality of sleep, and so on.

Self-Investigation: Level of self-awareness this week—discovery, examination, and personal development through reading and writing, expansion of personal knowledge, self-communication, and so on.

Creativity/Entertainment: Level of adventure, enjoyment of hobbies, art, laughter, amusement, and so on this week.

Relationships: Level of communication this week—with family, friends, my community, and so on.

Work/Education: Level of investment in work, career, homemaking (management of the household), and education this week.

Goal Setter	My goal(s) for next week are... Describe EATs.	What step(s) will I take next week to achieve my goal(s)?
Gratitude and Forgiveness		
Health		
Self-Investigation		
Creativity/ Entertainment		
Relationships		
Work/ Education		

Life is a melody, and you are the composer.

Date_____Time_____

Tip: With your eyes closed, take a few slow, deep inhalations and exhalations.
Review your day, open your eyes, and begin.

1. **Today**, after reviewing my day, what **E**motions, **A**ctions/behaviors, and **T**houghts (**EAT**s) arise?

2. **Today**, what made (and still makes) me happy? Describe **EAT**s.

3. **Today**, how did I love myself? Describe **EAT**s.

4. **Today**, how did I love others? Describe **EAT**s.

5. **Today**, what did I learn about myself? What did I learn in general? Describe the **EAT**s created from the lessons.

6. **Today**, did I accomplish the goal(s) I set for myself yesterday? (Yes/No) If not, what steps will I take to accomplish them?
   What is/are my goal(s) for tomorrow?
   By accomplishing my goal(s), what will it/they allow me to achieve?
   How will my goal(s) influence my **EAT**s?

7. **Today**, for whom and for what am I grateful? Describe the reasons. Describe **EAT**s.

There are two ways of spreading light: to be
the candle or the mirror that reflects it.
—EDITH WHARTON

Date_____**Time**_____

Tip: With your eyes closed, take a few slow, deep inhalations and exhalations. Review your day, open your eyes, and begin.

1. **Today**, after reviewing my day, what **E**motions, **A**ctions/behaviors, and **T**houghts (**EAT**s) arise?

2. **Today**, what made (and still makes) me happy? Describe **EAT**s.

3. **Today**, how did I love myself? Describe **EAT**s.

4. **Today**, how did I love others? Describe **EAT**s.

5. **Today**, what did I learn about myself? What did I learn in general? Describe the **EAT**s created from the lessons.

6. **Today**, did I accomplish the goal(s) I set for myself yesterday? (Yes/No) If not, what steps will I take to accomplish them?
   What is/are my goal(s) for tomorrow?
   By accomplishing my goal(s), what will it/they allow me to achieve?
   How will my goal(s) influence my **EAT**s?

7. **Today**, for whom and for what am I grateful? Describe the reasons. Describe **EAT**s.

Do what you can, with what you have, where you are.
—THEODORE ROOSEVELT

Date_____Time_____

Tip: With your eyes closed, take a few slow, deep inhalations and exhalations. Review your day, open your eyes, and begin.

1. **Today**, after reviewing my day, what **E**motions, **A**ctions/behaviors, and **T**houghts (**EAT**s) arise?

2. **Today**, what made (and still makes) me happy? Describe **EAT**s.

3. **Today**, how did I love myself? Describe **EAT**s.

4. **Today**, how did I love others? Describe **EAT**s.

5. **Today**, what did I learn about myself? What did I learn in general? Describe the **EAT**s created from the lessons.

6. **Today**, did I accomplish the goal(s) I set for myself yesterday? (Yes/No) If not, what steps will I take to accomplish them?
   What is/are my goal(s) for tomorrow?
   By accomplishing my goal(s), what will it/they allow me to achieve?
   How will my goal(s) influence my **EAT**s?

7. **Today**, for whom and for what am I grateful? Describe the reasons. Describe **EAT**s.

You are never given a dream without also
being given the power to make it true.
—Richard Bach

Date_____**Time**_____

Tip: With your eyes closed, take a few slow, deep inhalations and exhalations. Review your day, open your eyes, and begin.

1. **Today**, after reviewing my day, what **E**motions, **A**ctions/behaviors, and **T**houghts (**EAT**s) arise?

2. **Today**, what made (and still makes) me happy? Describe **EAT**s.

3. **Today**, how did I love myself? Describe **EAT**s.

4. **Today**, how did I love others? Describe **EAT**s.

5. **Today**, what did I learn about myself? What did I learn in general? Describe the **EAT**s created from the lessons.

6. **Today**, did I accomplish the goal(s) I set for myself yesterday? (Yes/No) If not, what steps will I take to accomplish them?
What is/are my goal(s) for tomorrow?
By accomplishing my goal(s), what will it/they allow me to achieve?
How will my goal(s) influence my **EAT**s?

7. **Today**, for whom and for what am I grateful? Describe the reasons. Describe **EAT**s.

It is during our darkest moments that
we must focus to see the light.
—ARISTOTLE

Date_____**Time**_____

Tip: With your eyes closed, take a few slow, deep inhalations and exhalations.
Review your day, open your eyes, and begin.

1. **Today**, after reviewing my day, what **E**motions, **A**ctions/behaviors, and **T**houghts (**EAT**s) arise?

2. **Today**, what made (and still makes) me happy? Describe **EAT**s.

3. **Today**, how did I love myself? Describe **EAT**s.

4. **Today**, how did I love others? Describe **EAT**s.

5. **Today**, what did I learn about myself? What did I learn in general? Describe the **EAT**s created from the lessons.

6. **Today**, did I accomplish the goal(s) I set for myself yesterday? (Yes/No) If not, what steps will I take to accomplish them?
What is/are my goal(s) for tomorrow?
By accomplishing my goal(s), what will it/they allow me to achieve?
How will my goal(s) influence my **EAT**s?

7. **Today**, for whom and for what am I grateful? Describe the reasons. Describe **EAT**s.

Once you expect something it will come.
—ABRAHAM HICKS

Date_____Time_____

Tip: With your eyes closed, take a few slow, deep inhalations and exhalations.
Review your day, open your eyes, and begin.

1. **Today**, after reviewing my day, what **E**motions, **A**ctions/behaviors, and **T**houghts (**EAT**s) arise?

2. **Today**, what made (and still makes) me happy? Describe **EAT**s.

3. **Today**, how did I love myself? Describe **EAT**s.

4. **Today**, how did I love others? Describe **EAT**s.

5. **Today**, what did I learn about myself? What did I learn in general? Describe the **EAT**s created from the lessons.

6. **Today**, did I accomplish the goal(s) I set for myself yesterday? (Yes/No) If not, what steps will I take to accomplish them?
   What is/are my goal(s) for tomorrow?
   By accomplishing my goal(s), what will it/they allow me to achieve?
   How will my goal(s) influence my **EAT**s?

7. **Today**, for whom and for what am I grateful? Describe the reasons. Describe **EAT**s.

Age is an issue of mind over matter. If
you don't mind, it doesn't matter.
—MARK TWAIN

Date_____**Time**_____

Tip: With your eyes closed, take a few slow, deep inhalations and exhalations.
Review your day, open your eyes, and begin.

1. **Today**, after reviewing my day, what **E**motions, **A**ctions/behaviors, and **T**houghts (**EAT**s) arise?

2. **Today**, what made (and still makes) me happy? Describe **EAT**s.

3. **Today**, how did I love myself? Describe **EAT**s.

4. **Today**, how did I love others? Describe **EAT**s.

5. **Today**, what did I learn about myself? What did I learn in general? Describe the **EAT**s created from the lessons.

6. **Today**, did I accomplish the goal(s) I set for myself yesterday? (Yes/No) If not, what steps will I take to accomplish them?
What is/are my goal(s) for tomorrow?
By accomplishing my goal(s), what will it/they allow me to achieve?
How will my goal(s) influence my **EAT**s?

7. **Today**, for whom and for what am I grateful? Describe the reasons. Describe **EAT**s.

A leader is one who knows the way,
goes the way, and shows the way.
—JOHN C. MAXWELL

Me

This Week's Melody

To further your self-discovery and self-awareness this week place music notes (♩) or dots on the music lines below. Each music note/dot will represent the tone/sound you chose to create in the following subjects this week:

♩The top position of the music note/dot on the music lines below represents a high level of fulfillment.

♩The middle position of the music note/dot on the music lines below represents a partial level of fulfillment.

♩The bottom position of the music note/dot on the music lines below represents a desire for further fulfillment.

Gratitude and Forgiveness: Level of thankfulness and forgiveness this week—gratitude and forgiveness for myself and others, using the events that happened *for* me this week.

Health: Level of body nourishment this week—healthy lifestyle, exercise, nutrition, meditation, quality of sleep, and so on.

Self-Investigation: Level of self-awareness this week—discovery, examination, and personal development through reading and writing, expansion of personal knowledge, self-communication, and so on.

Creativity/Entertainment: Level of adventure, enjoyment of hobbies, art, laughter, amusement, and so on this week.

Relationships: Level of communication this week—with family, friends, my community, and so on.

Work/Education: Level of investment in work, career, homemaking (management of the household), and education this week.

Goal Setter	My goal(s) for next week are... Describe EATs.	What step(s) will I take next week to achieve my goal(s)?
Gratitude and Forgiveness		
Health		
Self-Investigation		
Creativity/ Entertainment		
Relationships		
Work/ Education		

Life is a melody, and you are the composer.

Me

Date_____Time_____

Tip: With your eyes closed, take a few slow, deep inhalations and exhalations. Review your day, open your eyes, and begin.

1. **Today**, after reviewing my day, what **E**motions, **A**ctions/behaviors, and **T**houghts (**EAT**s) arise?

2. **Today**, what made (and still makes) me happy? Describe **EAT**s.

3. **Today**, how did I love myself? Describe **EAT**s.

4. **Today**, how did I love others? Describe **EAT**s.

5. **Today**, what did I learn about myself? What did I learn in general? Describe the **EAT**s created from the lessons.

6. **Today**, did I accomplish the goal(s) I set for myself yesterday? (Yes/No) If not, what steps will I take to accomplish them?
   What is/are my goal(s) for tomorrow?
   By accomplishing my goal(s), what will it/they allow me to achieve?
   How will my goal(s) influence my **EAT**s?

7. **Today**, for whom and for what am I grateful? Describe the reasons. Describe **EAT**s.

There is no failure except in no longer trying.
—ELBERT HUBBARD

Date_____Time_____

Tip: With your eyes closed, take a few slow, deep inhalations and exhalations.
Review your day, open your eyes, and begin.

1. Today, after reviewing my day, what **E**motions, **A**ctions/behaviors, and **T**houghts (**EAT**s) arise?

2. Today, what made (and still makes) me happy? Describe **EAT**s.

3. Today, how did I love myself? Describe **EAT**s.

4. Today, how did I love others? Describe **EAT**s.

5. **Today**, what did I learn about myself? What did I learn in general? Describe the **EAT**s created from the lessons.

6. **Today**, did I accomplish the goal(s) I set for myself yesterday? (Yes/No) If not, what steps will I take to accomplish them?
What is/are my goal(s) for tomorrow?
By accomplishing my goal(s), what will it/they allow me to achieve?
How will my goal(s) influence my **EAT**s?

7. **Today**, for whom and for what am I grateful? Describe the reasons. Describe **EAT**s.

Don't cry because it's over, smile because it happened.
—Dr. Seuss

Me

Date_____**Time**_____

Tip: With your eyes closed, take a few slow, deep inhalations and exhalations.
Review your day, open your eyes, and begin.

1. **Today**, after reviewing my day, what **E**motions, **A**ctions/behaviors, and **T**houghts (**EAT**s) arise?

2. **Today**, what made (and still makes) me happy? Describe **EAT**s.

3. **Today**, how did I love myself? Describe **EAT**s.

4. **Today**, how did I love others? Describe **EAT**s.

5. **Today**, what did I learn about myself? What did I learn in general? Describe the **EAT**s created from the lessons.

6. **Today**, did I accomplish the goal(s) I set for myself yesterday? (Yes/No) If not, what steps will I take to accomplish them?
What is/are my goal(s) for tomorrow?
By accomplishing my goal(s), what will it/they allow me to achieve?
How will my goal(s) influence my **EAT**s?

7. **Today**, for whom and for what am I grateful? Describe the reasons. Describe **EAT**s.

Victory is always possible for the
person who refuses to give up.
—NAPOLEON HILL

Date_____Time_____

Tip: With your eyes closed, take a few slow, deep inhalations and exhalations. Review your day, open your eyes, and begin.

1. **Today**, after reviewing my day, what **E**motions, **A**ctions/behaviors, and **T**houghts (**EAT**s) arise?

2. **Today**, what made (and still makes) me happy? Describe **EAT**s.

3. **Today**, how did I love myself? Describe **EAT**s.

4. **Today**, how did I love others? Describe **EAT**s.

5. **Today**, what did I learn about myself? What did I learn in general? Describe the **EAT**s created from the lessons.

6. **Today**, did I accomplish the goal(s) I set for myself yesterday? (Yes/No) If not, what steps will I take to accomplish them?
    What is/are my goal(s) for tomorrow?
    By accomplishing my goal(s), what will it/they allow me to achieve?
    How will my goal(s) influence my **EAT**s?

7. **Today**, for whom and for what am I grateful? Describe the reasons. Describe **EAT**s.

The secret of success is constancy to purpose.
—Benjamin Disraeli

Date_____Time_____

Tip: With your eyes closed, take a few slow, deep inhalations and exhalations. Review your day, open your eyes, and begin.

1. **Today**, after reviewing my day, what **E**motions, **A**ctions/behaviors, and **T**houghts (**EAT**s) arise?

2. **Today**, what made (and still makes) me happy? Describe **EAT**s.

3. **Today**, how did I love myself? Describe **EAT**s.

4. **Today**, how did I love others? Describe **EAT**s.

5. **Today**, what did I learn about myself? What did I learn in general? Describe the **EAT**s created from the lessons.

6. **Today**, did I accomplish the goal(s) I set for myself yesterday? (Yes/No) If not, what steps will I take to accomplish them?
What is/are my goal(s) for tomorrow?
By accomplishing my goal(s), what will it/they allow me to achieve?
How will my goal(s) influence my **EAT**s?

7. **Today**, for whom and for what am I grateful? Describe the reasons. Describe **EAT**s.

Hidden behind your fears and your
failures is the success you seek.
—ROBERT G. ALLEN

Date_____Time_____
Tip: With your eyes closed, take a few slow, deep inhalations and exhalations.
Review your day, open your eyes, and begin.

1. **Today**, after reviewing my day, what **E**motions, **A**ctions/behaviors, and **T**houghts (**EAT**s) arise?

2. **Today**, what made (and still makes) me happy? Describe **EAT**s.

3. **Today**, how did I love myself? Describe **EAT**s.

4. **Today**, how did I love others? Describe **EAT**s.

5. **Today**, what did I learn about myself? What did I learn in general? Describe the **EAT**s created from the lessons.

6. **Today**, did I accomplish the goal(s) I set for myself yesterday? (Yes/No) If not, what steps will I take to accomplish them?
   What is/are my goal(s) for tomorrow?
   By accomplishing my goal(s), what will it/they allow me to achieve?
   How will my goal(s) influence my **EAT**s?

7. **Today**, for whom and for what am I grateful? Describe the reasons. Describe **EAT**s.

Doing what you love is the cornerstone
of having abundance in your life.
—Dr. Wayne Dyer

Date_____**Time**_____

Tip: With your eyes closed, take a few slow, deep inhalations and exhalations.
Review your day, open your eyes, and begin.

1. **Today**, after reviewing my day, what **E**motions, **A**ctions/behaviors, and **T**houghts (**EAT**s) arise?

2. **Today**, what made (and still makes) me happy? Describe **EAT**s.

3. **Today**, how did I love myself? Describe **EAT**s.

4. **Today**, how did I love others? Describe **EAT**s.

5. **Today**, what did I learn about myself? What did I learn in general? Describe the **EAT**s created from the lessons.

6. **Today**, did I accomplish the goal(s) I set for myself yesterday? (Yes/No) If not, what steps will I take to accomplish them?
What is/are my goal(s) for tomorrow?
By accomplishing my goal(s), what will it/they allow me to achieve?
How will my goal(s) influence my **EAT**s?

7. **Today**, for whom and for what am I grateful? Describe the reasons. Describe **EAT**s.

There is no way to happiness - happiness is the way.
—THICH NHAT HANH

This Week's Melody

To further your self-discovery and self-awareness this week place music notes (♩) or dots on the music lines below. Each music note/dot will represent the tone/sound you chose to create in the following subjects this week:

♩The top position of the music note/dot on the music lines below represents a high level of fulfillment.

♩The middle position of the music note/dot on the music lines below represents a partial level of fulfillment.

♩The bottom position of the music note/dot on the music lines below represents a desire for further fulfillment.

Gratitude and Forgiveness: Level of thankfulness and forgiveness this week—gratitude and forgiveness for myself and others, using the events that happened *for* me this week.

Health: Level of body nourishment this week—healthy lifestyle, exercise, nutrition, meditation, quality of sleep, and so on.

Self-Investigation: Level of self-awareness this week—discovery, examination, and personal development through reading and writing, expansion of personal knowledge, self-communication, and so on.

Creativity/Entertainment: Level of adventure, enjoyment of hobbies, art, laughter, amusement, and so on this week.

Relationships: Level of communication this week—with family, friends, my community, and so on.

Work/Education: Level of investment in work, career, homemaking (management of the household), and education this week.

Goal Setter	My goal(s) for next week are... Describe EATs.	What step(s) will I take next week to achieve my goal(s)?
Gratitude and Forgiveness		
Health		
Self-Investigation		
Creativity/ Entertainment		
Relationships		
Work/ Education		

Life is a melody, and you are the composer.

Date_____**Time**_____

Tip: With your eyes closed, take a few slow, deep inhalations and exhalations.
Review your day, open your eyes, and begin.

1. **Today**, after reviewing my day, what **E**motions, **A**ctions/behaviors, and **T**houghts (**EAT**s) arise?

2. **Today**, what made (and still makes) me happy? Describe **EAT**s.

3. **Today**, how did I love myself? Describe **EAT**s.

4. **Today**, how did I love others? Describe **EAT**s.

5. **Today**, what did I learn about myself? What did I learn in general? Describe the **EAT**s created from the lessons.

6. **Today**, did I accomplish the goal(s) I set for myself yesterday? (Yes/No) If not, what steps will I take to accomplish them?
What is/are my goal(s) for tomorrow?
By accomplishing my goal(s), what will it/they allow me to achieve?
How will my goal(s) influence my **EAT**s?

7. **Today**, for whom and for what am I grateful? Describe the reasons. Describe **EAT**s.

One of the secrets to success is to refuse
to let temporary setbacks defeat us.
—MARY KAY ASH

Date_____Time_____

Tip: With your eyes closed, take a few slow, deep inhalations and exhalations.
Review your day, open your eyes, and begin.

1. **Today**, after reviewing my day, what **E**motions, **A**ctions/behaviors, and **T**houghts (**EAT**s) arise?

2. **Today**, what made (and still makes) me happy? Describe **EAT**s.

3. **Today**, how did I love myself? Describe **EAT**s.

4. **Today**, how did I love others? Describe **EAT**s.

5. **Today**, what did I learn about myself? What did I learn in general? Describe the **EAT**s created from the lessons.

6. **Today**, did I accomplish the goal(s) I set for myself yesterday? (Yes/No) If not, what steps will I take to accomplish them?
What is/are my goal(s) for tomorrow?
By accomplishing my goal(s), what will it/they allow me to achieve?
How will my goal(s) influence my **EAT**s?

7. **Today**, for whom and for what am I grateful? Describe the reasons. Describe **EAT**s.

Take care of your body. It's the only
place you have to live.
—Jim Rohn

Date_____Time_____

Tip: With your eyes closed, take a few slow, deep inhalations and exhalations.
Review your day, open your eyes, and begin.

1. **Today**, after reviewing my day, what **E**motions, **A**ctions/behaviors, and **T**houghts (**EAT**s) arise?

2. **Today**, what made (and still makes) me happy? Describe **EAT**s.

3. **Today**, how did I love myself? Describe **EAT**s.

4. **Today**, how did I love others? Describe **EAT**s.

5. **Today**, what did I learn about myself? What did I learn in general? Describe the **EAT**s created from the lessons.

6. **Today**, did I accomplish the goal(s) I set for myself yesterday? (Yes/No) If not, what steps will I take to accomplish them?
What is/are my goal(s) for tomorrow?
By accomplishing my goal(s), what will it/they allow me to achieve?
How will my goal(s) influence my **EAT**s?

7. **Today**, for whom and for what am I grateful? Describe the reasons. Describe **EAT**s.

Every day may not be good...but there's
something good in every day.
—Alice Morse Earle

Date_____**Time**_____

Tip: With your eyes closed, take a few slow, deep inhalations and exhalations.
Review your day, open your eyes, and begin.

1. **Today**, after reviewing my day, what **E**motions, **A**ctions/behaviors, and **T**houghts (**EAT**s) arise?

2. **Today**, what made (and still makes) me happy? Describe **EAT**s.

3. **Today**, how did I love myself? Describe **EAT**s.

4. **Today**, how did I love others? Describe **EAT**s.

5. **Today**, what did I learn about myself? What did I learn in general? Describe the **EAT**s created from the lessons.

6. **Today**, did I accomplish the goal(s) I set for myself yesterday? (Yes/No) If not, what steps will I take to accomplish them?
What is/are my goal(s) for tomorrow?
By accomplishing my goal(s), what will it/they allow me to achieve?
How will my goal(s) influence my **EAT**s?

7. **Today**, for whom and for what am I grateful? Describe the reasons. Describe **EAT**s.

The best way to predict your future is to create it.
—ABRAHAM LINCOLN

Date_____Time_____

Tip: With your eyes closed, take a few slow, deep inhalations and exhalations. Review your day, open your eyes, and begin.

1. **Today**, after reviewing my day, what **E**motions, **A**ctions/behaviors, and **T**houghts (**EAT**s) arise?

2. **Today**, what made (and still makes) me happy? Describe **EAT**s.

3. **Today**, how did I love myself? Describe **EAT**s.

4. **Today**, how did I love others? Describe **EAT**s.

5. **Today**, what did I learn about myself? What did I learn in general? Describe the **EAT**s created from the lessons.

6. **Today**, did I accomplish the goal(s) I set for myself yesterday? (Yes/No) If not, what steps will I take to accomplish them?
What is/are my goal(s) for tomorrow?
By accomplishing my goal(s), what will it/they allow me to achieve?
How will my goal(s) influence my **EAT**s?

7. **Today**, for whom and for what am I grateful? Describe the reasons. Describe **EAT**s.

Knowing yourself is the beginning of all wisdom.
—Aristotle

Me

Date_____Time_____

Tip: With your eyes closed, take a few slow, deep inhalations and exhalations. Review your day, open your eyes, and begin.

1. **Today**, after reviewing my day, what **E**motions, **A**ctions/behaviors, and **T**houghts (**EAT**s) arise?

2. **Today**, what made (and still makes) me happy? Describe **EAT**s.

3. **Today**, how did I love myself? Describe **EAT**s.

4. **Today**, how did I love others? Describe **EAT**s.

5. **Today**, what did I learn about myself? What did I learn in general? Describe the **EAT**s created from the lessons.

6. **Today**, did I accomplish the goal(s) I set for myself yesterday? (Yes/No) If not, what steps will I take to accomplish them?
What is/are my goal(s) for tomorrow?
By accomplishing my goal(s), what will it/they allow me to achieve?
How will my goal(s) influence my **EAT**s?

7. **Today**, for whom and for what am I grateful? Describe the reasons. Describe **EAT**s.

Failure is simply the opportunity to begin
again, this time more intelligently.
—HENRY FORD

Date_____Time_____

Tip: With your eyes closed, take a few slow, deep inhalations and exhalations. Review your day, open your eyes, and begin.

1. **Today**, after reviewing my day, what **E**motions, **A**ctions/behaviors, and **T**houghts (**EAT**s) arise?

2. **Today**, what made (and still makes) me happy? Describe **EAT**s.

3. **Today**, how did I love myself? Describe **EAT**s.

4. **Today**, how did I love others? Describe **EAT**s.

5. **Today**, what did I learn about myself? What did I learn in general? Describe the **EAT**s created from the lessons.

6. **Today**, did I accomplish the goal(s) I set for myself yesterday? (Yes/No) If not, what steps will I take to accomplish them? What is/are my goal(s) for tomorrow? By accomplishing my goal(s), what will it/they allow me to achieve? How will my goal(s) influence my **EAT**s?

7. **Today**, for whom and for what am I grateful? Describe the reasons. Describe **EAT**s.

I found that If you love life, life will love you back.
—ARTHUR RUBINSTEIN

This Week's Melody

To further your self-discovery and self-awareness this week place music notes (♩) or dots on the music lines below. Each music note/dot will represent the tone/sound you chose to create in the following subjects this week:

♩The top position of the music note/dot on the music lines below represents a high level of fulfillment.

♩The middle position of the music note/dot on the music lines below represents a partial level of fulfillment.

♩The bottom position of the music note/dot on the music lines below represents a desire for further fulfillment.

Gratitude and Forgiveness: Level of thankfulness and forgiveness this week—gratitude and forgiveness for myself and others, using the events that happened *for* me this week.

Health: Level of body nourishment this week—healthy lifestyle, exercise, nutrition, meditation, quality of sleep, and so on.

Self-Investigation: Level of self-awareness this week—discovery, examination, and personal development through reading and writing, expansion of personal knowledge, self-communication, and so on.

Creativity/Entertainment: Level of adventure, enjoyment of hobbies, art, laughter, amusement, and so on this week.

Relationships: Level of communication this week—with family, friends, my community, and so on.

Work/Education: Level of investment in work, career, homemaking (management of the household), and education this week.

Goal Setter	My goal(s) for next week are... Describe EATs.	What step(s) will I take next week to achieve my goal(s)?
Gratitude and Forgiveness		
Health		
Self-Investigation		
Creativity/ Entertainment		
Relationships		
Work/ Education		

Life is a melody, and you are the composer.

Date_____Time_____

Tip: With your eyes closed, take a few slow, deep inhalations and exhalations.
Review your day, open your eyes, and begin.

1. **Today**, after reviewing my day, what **E**motions, **A**ctions/behaviors, and **T**houghts (**EAT**s) arise?

2. **Today**, what made (and still makes) me happy? Describe **EAT**s.

3. **Today**, how did I love myself? Describe **EAT**s.

4. **Today**, how did I love others? Describe **EAT**s.

5. **Today**, what did I learn about myself? What did I learn in general? Describe the **EAT**s created from the lessons.

6. **Today**, did I accomplish the goal(s) I set for myself yesterday? (Yes/No) If not, what steps will I take to accomplish them?
   What is/are my goal(s) for tomorrow?
   By accomplishing my goal(s), what will it/they allow me to achieve?
   How will my goal(s) influence my **EAT**s?

7. **Today**, for whom and for what am I grateful? Describe the reasons. Describe **EAT**s.

Obstacles are those frightful things you see
when you take your eyes off your goal.
—HENRY FORD

Date_____**Time**_____

Tip: With your eyes closed, take a few slow, deep inhalations and exhalations.
Review your day, open your eyes, and begin.

1. **Today**, after reviewing my day, what **E**motions, **A**ctions/behaviors, and **T**houghts (**EAT**s) arise?

2. **Today**, what made (and still makes) me happy? Describe **EAT**s.

3. **Today**, how did I love myself? Describe **EAT**s.

4. **Today**, how did I love others? Describe **EAT**s.

5. **Today**, what did I learn about myself? What did I learn in general? Describe the **EAT**s created from the lessons.

6. **Today**, did I accomplish the goal(s) I set for myself yesterday? (Yes/No) If not, what steps will I take to accomplish them?
   What is/are my goal(s) for tomorrow?
   By accomplishing my goal(s), what will it/they allow me to achieve?
   How will my goal(s) influence my **EAT**s?

7. **Today**, for whom and for what am I grateful? Describe the reasons. Describe **EAT**s.

You can never cross the ocean until you have
the courage to lose sight of the shore.
—CHRISTOPHER COLUMBUS

Date_____Time_____

Tip: With your eyes closed, take a few slow, deep inhalations and exhalations.
Review your day, open your eyes, and begin.

1. **Today**, after reviewing my day, what **E**motions, **A**ctions/behaviors, and **T**houghts (**EAT**s) arise?

2. **Today**, what made (and still makes) me happy? Describe **EAT**s.

3. **Today**, how did I love myself? Describe **EAT**s.

4. **Today**, how did I love others? Describe **EAT**s.

5. **Today**, what did I learn about myself? What did I learn in general? Describe the **EAT**s created from the lessons.

6. **Today**, did I accomplish the goal(s) I set for myself yesterday? (Yes/No) If not, what steps will I take to accomplish them?
What is/are my goal(s) for tomorrow?
By accomplishing my goal(s), what will it/they allow me to achieve?
How will my goal(s) influence my **EAT**s?

7. **Today**, for whom and for what am I grateful? Describe the reasons. Describe **EAT**s.

Change your thoughts and you change your world.
—NORMAN VINCENT PHIL

Date_____Time_____

Tip: With your eyes closed, take a few slow, deep inhalations and exhalations. Review your day, open your eyes, and begin.

1. **Today**, after reviewing my day, what **E**motions, **A**ctions/behaviors, and **T**houghts (**EAT**s) arise?

2. **Today**, what made (and still makes) me happy? Describe **EAT**s.

3. **Today**, how did I love myself? Describe **EAT**s.

4. **Today**, how did I love others? Describe **EAT**s.

5. **Today**, what did I learn about myself? What did I learn in general? Describe the **EAT**s created from the lessons.

6. **Today**, did I accomplish the goal(s) I set for myself yesterday? (Yes/No) If not, what steps will I take to accomplish them?
What is/are my goal(s) for tomorrow?
By accomplishing my goal(s), what will it/they allow me to achieve?
How will my goal(s) influence my **EAT**s?

7. **Today**, for whom and for what am I grateful? Describe the reasons. Describe **EAT**s.

Strength doesn't come from what you can do. It comes
from overcoming the things you once thought you couldn't.
—RIKKI ROGERS

Date_____**Time**_____

Tip: With your eyes closed, take a few slow, deep inhalations and exhalations. Review your day, open your eyes, and begin.

1. **Today**, after reviewing my day, what **E**motions, **A**ctions/behaviors, and **T**houghts (**EAT**s) arise?

2. **Today**, what made (and still makes) me happy? Describe **EAT**s.

3. **Today**, how did I love myself? Describe **EAT**s.

4. **Today**, how did I love others? Describe **EAT**s.

5. **Today**, what did I learn about myself? What did I learn in general? Describe the **EAT**s created from the lessons.

6. **Today**, did I accomplish the goal(s) I set for myself yesterday? (Yes/No) If not, what steps will I take to accomplish them?
   What is/are my goal(s) for tomorrow?
   By accomplishing my goal(s), what will it/they allow me to achieve?
   How will my goal(s) influence my **EAT**s?

7. **Today**, for whom and for what am I grateful? Describe the reasons. Describe **EAT**s.

Patience is a necessary ingredient of genius.
—Benjamin Disraeli

Date_____**Time**_____

Tip: With your eyes closed, take a few slow, deep inhalations and exhalations.
Review your day, open your eyes, and begin.

1. **Today**, after reviewing my day, what **E**motions, **A**ctions/behaviors, and **T**houghts (**EAT**s) arise?

2. **Today**, what made (and still makes) me happy? Describe **EAT**s.

3. **Today**, how did I love myself? Describe **EAT**s.

4. **Today**, how did I love others? Describe **EAT**s.

5. **Today**, what did I learn about myself? What did I learn in general? Describe the **EAT**s created from the lessons.

6. **Today**, did I accomplish the goal(s) I set for myself yesterday? (Yes/No) If not, what steps will I take to accomplish them?
What is/are my goal(s) for tomorrow?
By accomplishing my goal(s), what will it/they allow me to achieve?
How will my goal(s) influence my **EAT**s?

7. **Today**, for whom and for what am I grateful? Describe the reasons. Describe **EAT**s.

Believe you can and you're half way there.
—THEODORE ROOSEVELT

Date_____Time_____

Tip: With your eyes closed, take a few slow, deep inhalations and exhalations. Review your day, open your eyes, and begin.

1. **Today**, after reviewing my day, what **E**motions, **A**ctions/behaviors, and **T**houghts (**EAT**s) arise?

2. **Today**, what made (and still makes) me happy? Describe **EAT**s.

3. **Today**, how did I love myself? Describe **EAT**s.

4. **Today**, how did I love others? Describe **EAT**s.

5. **Today**, what did I learn about myself? What did I learn in general? Describe the **EAT**s created from the lessons.

6. **Today**, did I accomplish the goal(s) I set for myself yesterday? (Yes/No) If not, what steps will I take to accomplish them?
What is/are my goal(s) for tomorrow?
By accomplishing my goal(s), what will it/they allow me to achieve?
How will my goal(s) influence my **EAT**s?

7. **Today**, for whom and for what am I grateful? Describe the reasons. Describe **EAT**s.

A pessimist sees the difficulty in every opportunity;
an optimist sees the opportunity in every difficulty.
—Winston Churchill

Me

This Week's Melody

To further your self-discovery and self-awareness this week place music notes (♩) or dots on the music lines below. Each music note/dot will represent the tone/sound you chose to create in the following subjects this week:

♩The top position of the music note/dot on the music lines below represents a high level of fulfillment.
♩The middle position of the music note/dot on the music lines below represents a partial level of fulfillment.
♩The bottom position of the music note/dot on the music lines below represents a desire for further fulfillment.

Gratitude and Forgiveness	Health	Self-Investigation	Creativity/Entertainment	Relationships	Work/Education

Gratitude and Forgiveness: Level of thankfulness and forgiveness this week—gratitude and forgiveness for myself and others, using the events that happened *for* me this week.

Health: Level of body nourishment this week—healthy lifestyle, exercise, nutrition, meditation, quality of sleep, and so on.

Self-Investigation: Level of self-awareness this week—discovery, examination, and personal development through reading and writing, expansion of personal knowledge, self-communication, and so on.

Creativity/Entertainment: Level of adventure, enjoyment of hobbies, art, laughter, amusement, and so on this week.

Relationships: Level of communication this week—with family, friends, my community, and so on.

Work/Education: Level of investment in work, career, homemaking (management of the household), and education this week.

Goal Setter	My goal(s) for next week are... Describe EATs.	What step(s) will I take next week to achieve my goal(s)?
Gratitude and Forgiveness		
Health		
Self-Investigation		
Creativity/ Entertainment		
Relationships		
Work/ Education		

Life is a melody, and you are the composer.

Date_____**Time**_____

Tip: With your eyes closed, take a few slow, deep inhalations and exhalations.
Review your day, open your eyes, and begin.

1. **Today**, after reviewing my day, what **E**motions, **A**ctions/behaviors, and **T**houghts (**EAT**s) arise?

2. **Today**, what made (and still makes) me happy? Describe **EAT**s.

3. **Today**, how did I love myself? Describe **EAT**s.

4. **Today**, how did I love others? Describe **EAT**s.

5. **Today**, what did I learn about myself? What did I learn in general? Describe the **EAT**s created from the lessons.

6. **Today**, did I accomplish the goal(s) I set for myself yesterday? (Yes/No) If not, what steps will I take to accomplish them?
What is/are my goal(s) for tomorrow?
By accomplishing my goal(s), what will it/they allow me to achieve?
How will my goal(s) influence my **EAT**s?

7. **Today**, for whom and for what am I grateful? Describe the reasons. Describe **EAT**s.

Smile in the mirror. Do that every morning and
you'll start to see a big difference in your life.
—YOKO ONO

Date_____Time_____

Tip: With your eyes closed, take a few slow, deep inhalations and exhalations.
Review your day, open your eyes, and begin.

1. **Today**, after reviewing my day, what **E**motions, **A**ctions/behaviors, and **T**houghts (**EAT**s) arise?

2. **Today**, what made (and still makes) me happy? Describe **EAT**s.

3. **Today**, how did I love myself? Describe **EAT**s.

4. **Today**, how did I love others? Describe **EAT**s.

5. **Today**, what did I learn about myself? What did I learn in general? Describe the **EAT**s created from the lessons.

6. **Today**, did I accomplish the goal(s) I set for myself yesterday? (Yes/No) If not, what steps will I take to accomplish them?
   What is/are my goal(s) for tomorrow?
   By accomplishing my goal(s), what will it/they allow me to achieve?
   How will my goal(s) influence my **EAT**s?

7. **Today**, for whom and for what am I grateful? Describe the reasons. Describe **EAT**s.

Either you run the day or the day runs you.
— JIM ROHN

Date_____Time_____

Tip: With your eyes closed, take a few slow, deep inhalations and exhalations.
Review your day, open your eyes, and begin.

1. **Today**, after reviewing my day, what **E**motions, **A**ctions/behaviors, and **T**houghts (**EAT**s) arise?

2. **Today**, what made (and still makes) me happy? Describe **EAT**s.

3. **Today**, how did I love myself? Describe **EAT**s.

4. **Today**, how did I love others? Describe **EAT**s.

5. **Today**, what did I learn about myself? What did I learn in general? Describe the **EAT**s created from the lessons.

6. **Today**, did I accomplish the goal(s) I set for myself yesterday? (Yes/No) If not, what steps will I take to accomplish them?
What is/are my goal(s) for tomorrow?
By accomplishing my goal(s), what will it/they allow me to achieve?
How will my goal(s) influence my **EAT**s?

7. **Today**, for whom and for what am I grateful? Describe the reasons. Describe **EAT**s.

What I am looking for is not out there, it is in me.
—HELEN KELLER

Date_____Time_____

Tip: With your eyes closed, take a few slow, deep inhalations and exhalations.
Review your day, open your eyes, and begin.

1. **Today**, after reviewing my day, what **E**motions, **A**ctions/behaviors, and **T**houghts (**EAT**s) arise?

2. **Today**, what made (and still makes) me happy? Describe **EAT**s.

3. **Today**, how did I love myself? Describe **EAT**s.

4. **Today**, how did I love others? Describe **EAT**s.

5. **Today**, what did I learn about myself? What did I learn in general? Describe the **EAT**s created from the lessons.

6. **Today**, did I accomplish the goal(s) I set for myself yesterday? (Yes/No) If not, what steps will I take to accomplish them?
What is/are my goal(s) for tomorrow?
By accomplishing my goal(s), what will it/they allow me to achieve?
How will my goal(s) influence my **EAT**s?

7. **Today**, for whom and for what am I grateful? Describe the reasons. Describe **EAT**s.

Some people want it to happen, some wish it
would happen, others make it happen.
—MICHAEL JORDAN

Date_____Time_____

Tip: With your eyes closed, take a few slow, deep inhalations and exhalations.
Review your day, open your eyes, and begin.

1. **Today**, after reviewing my day, what **E**motions, **A**ctions/behaviors, and **T**houghts (**EAT**s) arise?

2. **Today**, what made (and still makes) me happy? Describe **EAT**s.

3. **Today**, how did I love myself? Describe **EAT**s.

4. **Today**, how did I love others? Describe **EAT**s.

5. **Today**, what did I learn about myself? What did I learn in general? Describe the **EAT**s created from the lessons.

6. **Today**, did I accomplish the goal(s) I set for myself yesterday? (Yes/No) If not, what steps will I take to accomplish them? What is/are my goal(s) for tomorrow? By accomplishing my goal(s), what will it/they allow me to achieve? How will my goal(s) influence my **EAT**s?

7. **Today**, for whom and for what am I grateful? Describe the reasons. Describe **EAT**s.

Experience is the teacher of all things.
—JULIUS CAESAR

Date_____Time_____

Tip: With your eyes closed, take a few slow, deep inhalations and exhalations.
Review your day, open your eyes, and begin.

1. **Today**, after reviewing my day, what **E**motions, **A**ctions/behaviors, and **T**houghts (**EAT**s) arise?

2. **Today**, what made (and still makes) me happy? Describe **EAT**s.

3. **Today**, how did I love myself? Describe **EAT**s.

4. **Today**, how did I love others? Describe **EAT**s.

5. **Today**, what did I learn about myself? What did I learn in general? Describe the **EAT**s created from the lessons.

6. **Today**, did I accomplish the goal(s) I set for myself yesterday? (Yes/No) If not, what steps will I take to accomplish them?
   What is/are my goal(s) for tomorrow?
   By accomplishing my goal(s), what will it/they allow me to achieve?
   How will my goal(s) influence my **EAT**s?

7. **Today**, for whom and for what am I grateful? Describe the reasons. Describe **EAT**s.

Every obstacle is a test.
—WAYNE DYER

Date_____Time_____

Tip: With your eyes closed, take a few slow, deep inhalations and exhalations. Review your day, open your eyes, and begin.

1. **Today**, after reviewing my day, what **E**motions, **A**ctions/behaviors, and **T**houghts (**EAT**s) arise?

2. **Today**, what made (and still makes) me happy? Describe **EAT**s.

3. **Today**, how did I love myself? Describe **EAT**s.

4. **Today**, how did I love others? Describe **EAT**s.

5. **Today**, what did I learn about myself? What did I learn in general? Describe the **EAT**s created from the lessons.

6. **Today**, did I accomplish the goal(s) I set for myself yesterday? (Yes/No) If not, what steps will I take to accomplish them?
   What is/are my goal(s) for tomorrow?
   By accomplishing my goal(s), what will it/they allow me to achieve?
   How will my goal(s) influence my **EAT**s?

7. **Today**, for whom and for what am I grateful? Describe the reasons. Describe **EAT**s.

Tell me and I forget, teach me and I may
remember, involve me and I learn.
—Benjamin Franklin

This Week's Melody

To further your self-discovery and self-awareness this week place music notes (♪) or dots on the music lines below. Each music note/dot will represent the tone/sound you chose to create in the following subjects this week:

♪The top position of the music note/dot on the music lines below represents a high level of fulfillment.

♪The middle position of the music note/dot on the music lines below represents a partial level of fulfillment.

♪The bottom position of the music note/dot on the music lines below represents a desire for further fulfillment.

Gratitude and Forgiveness: Level of thankfulness and forgiveness this week—gratitude and forgiveness for myself and others, using the events that happened *for* me this week.

Health: Level of body nourishment this week—healthy lifestyle, exercise, nutrition, meditation, quality of sleep, and so on.

Self-Investigation: Level of self-awareness this week—discovery, examination, and personal development through reading and writing, expansion of personal knowledge, self-communication, and so on.

Creativity/Entertainment: Level of adventure, enjoyment of hobbies, art, laughter, amusement, and so on this week.

Relationships: Level of communication this week—with family, friends, my community, and so on.

Work/Education: Level of investment in work, career, homemaking (management of the household), and education this week.

Goal Setter	My goal(s) for next week are... Describe EATs.	What step(s) will I take next week to achieve my goal(s)?
Gratitude and Forgiveness		
Health		
Self-Investigation		
Creativity/ Entertainment		
Relationships		
Work/ Education		

Life is a melody, and you are the composer.

Date_____**Time**_____

Tip: With your eyes closed, take a few slow, deep inhalations and exhalations. Review your day, open your eyes, and begin.

1. **Today**, after reviewing my day, what **E**motions, **A**ctions/behaviors, and **T**houghts (**EAT**s) arise?

2. **Today**, what made (and still makes) me happy? Describe **EAT**s.

3. **Today**, how did I love myself? Describe **EAT**s.

4. **Today**, how did I love others? Describe **EAT**s.

5. **Today**, what did I learn about myself? What did I learn in general? Describe the **EAT**s created from the lessons.

6. **Today**, did I accomplish the goal(s) I set for myself yesterday? (Yes/No) If not, what steps will I take to accomplish them?
   What is/are my goal(s) for tomorrow?
   By accomplishing my goal(s), what will it/they allow me to achieve?
   How will my goal(s) influence my **EAT**s?

7. **Today**, for whom and for what am I grateful? Describe the reasons. Describe **EAT**s.

Until you make the unconscious conscious, it
will direct your life and you will call it fate.
—C.G. JUNG

Date_____Time_____

Tip: With your eyes closed, take a few slow, deep inhalations and exhalations.
Review your day, open your eyes, and begin.

1. **Today**, after reviewing my day, what **E**motions, **A**ctions/behaviors, and **T**houghts (**EAT**s) arise?

2. **Today**, what made (and still makes) me happy? Describe **EAT**s.

3. **Today**, how did I love myself? Describe **EAT**s.

4. **Today**, how did I love others? Describe **EAT**s.

5. **Today**, what did I learn about myself? What did I learn in general? Describe the **EAT**s created from the lessons.

6. **Today**, did I accomplish the goal(s) I set for myself yesterday? (Yes/No) If not, what steps will I take to accomplish them?
What is/are my goal(s) for tomorrow?
By accomplishing my goal(s), what will it/they allow me to achieve?
How will my goal(s) influence my **EAT**s?

7. **Today**, for whom and for what am I grateful? Describe the reasons. Describe **EAT**s.

The best way to predict the future is to create it.
—PETER DRUCKER

Me

Date_____**Time**_____

Tip: With your eyes closed, take a few slow, deep inhalations and exhalations. Review your day, open your eyes, and begin.

1. **Today**, after reviewing my day, what **E**motions, **A**ctions/behaviors, and **T**houghts (**EAT**s) arise?

2. **Today**, what made (and still makes) me happy? Describe **EAT**s.

3. **Today**, how did I love myself? Describe **EAT**s.

4. **Today**, how did I love others? Describe **EAT**s.

5. **Today**, what did I learn about myself? What did I learn in general? Describe the **EAT**s created from the lessons.

6. **Today**, did I accomplish the goal(s) I set for myself yesterday? (Yes/No) If not, what steps will I take to accomplish them?
What is/are my goal(s) for tomorrow?
By accomplishing my goal(s), what will it/they allow me to achieve?
How will my goal(s) influence my **EAT**s?

7. **Today**, for whom and for what am I grateful? Describe the reasons. Describe **EAT**s.

It is not how much we have, but how much
we enjoy, that makes happiness.
—CHARLES SPURGEON

Me

Date_____Time_____

Tip: With your eyes closed, take a few slow, deep inhalations and exhalations.
Review your day, open your eyes, and begin.

1. **Today**, after reviewing my day, what **E**motions, **A**ctions/behaviors, and **T**houghts (**EAT**s) arise?

2. **Today**, what made (and still makes) me happy? Describe **EAT**s.

3. **Today**, how did I love myself? Describe **EAT**s.

4. **Today**, how did I love others? Describe **EAT**s.

5. **Today**, what did I learn about myself? What did I learn in general? Describe the **EAT**s created from the lessons.

6. **Today**, did I accomplish the goal(s) I set for myself yesterday? (Yes/No) If not, what steps will I take to accomplish them? What is/are my goal(s) for tomorrow? By accomplishing my goal(s), what will it/they allow me to achieve? How will my goal(s) influence my **EAT**s?

7. **Today**, for whom and for what am I grateful? Describe the reasons. Describe **EAT**s.

Our greatest weakness lies in giving up. The most certain way to succeed is always to try just one more time.
—Thomas A. Edison

Me

Date_____Time_____

Tip: With your eyes closed, take a few slow, deep inhalations and exhalations.
Review your day, open your eyes, and begin.

1. **Today**, after reviewing my day, what **E**motions, **A**ctions/behaviors, and **T**houghts (**EAT**s) arise?

2. **Today**, what made (and still makes) me happy? Describe **EAT**s.

3. **Today**, how did I love myself? Describe **EAT**s.

4. **Today**, how did I love others? Describe **EAT**s.

5. **Today**, what did I learn about myself? What did I learn in general? Describe the **EAT**s created from the lessons.

6. **Today**, did I accomplish the goal(s) I set for myself yesterday? (Yes/No) If not, what steps will I take to accomplish them?
   What is/are my goal(s) for tomorrow?
   By accomplishing my goal(s), what will it/they allow me to achieve?
   How will my goal(s) influence my **EAT**s?

7. **Today**, for whom and for what am I grateful? Describe the reasons. Describe **EAT**s.

The most creative act you will ever undertake
is the act of creating yourself.
—DEEPAK CHOPRA

Date_____**Time**_____

Tip: With your eyes closed, take a few slow, deep inhalations and exhalations.
Review your day, open your eyes, and begin.

1. **Today**, after reviewing my day, what **E**motions, **A**ctions/behaviors, and **T**houghts (**EAT**s) arise?

2. **Today**, what made (and still makes) me happy? Describe **EAT**s.

3. **Today**, how did I love myself? Describe **EAT**s.

4. **Today**, how did I love others? Describe **EAT**s.

5. **Today**, what did I learn about myself? What did I learn in general? Describe the **EAT**s created from the lessons.

6. **Today**, did I accomplish the goal(s) I set for myself yesterday? (Yes/No) If not, what steps will I take to accomplish them?
    What is/are my goal(s) for tomorrow?
    By accomplishing my goal(s), what will it/they allow me to achieve?
    How will my goal(s) influence my **EAT**s?

7. **Today**, for whom and for what am I grateful? Describe the reasons. Describe **EAT**s.

Be kind whenever possible. It is always possible.
—DALAI LAMA

Date_____Time_____

Tip: With your eyes closed, take a few slow, deep inhalations and exhalations.
Review your day, open your eyes, and begin.

1. **Today**, after reviewing my day, what **E**motions, **A**ctions/behaviors, and **T**houghts (**EAT**s) arise?

2. **Today**, what made (and still makes) me happy? Describe **EAT**s.

3. **Today**, how did I love myself? Describe **EAT**s.

4. **Today**, how did I love others? Describe **EAT**s.

5. **Today**, what did I learn about myself? What did I learn in general?
   Describe the **EAT**s created from the lessons.

6. **Today**, did I accomplish the goal(s) I set for myself yesterday?
   (Yes/No) If not, what steps will I take to accomplish them?
   What is/are my goal(s) for tomorrow?
   By accomplishing my goal(s), what will it/they allow me to achieve?
   How will my goal(s) influence my **EAT**s?

7. **Today**, for whom and for what am I grateful? Describe the reasons. Describe **EAT**s.

Only you can control your future.
—Dr. Seuss

This Week's Melody

To further your self-discovery and self-awareness this week place music notes (♩) or dots on the music lines below. Each music note/dot will represent the tone/sound you chose to create in the following subjects this week:

♩The top position of the music note/dot on the music lines below represents a high level of fulfillment.

♩The middle position of the music note/dot on the music lines below represents a partial level of fulfillment.

♩The bottom position of the music note/dot on the music lines below represents a desire for further fulfillment.

	Gratitude and Forgiveness	Health	Self-Investigation	Creativity/Entertainment	Relationships	Work/Education

Gratitude and Forgiveness: Level of thankfulness and forgiveness this week—gratitude and forgiveness for myself and others, using the events that happened *for* me this week.

Health: Level of body nourishment this week—healthy lifestyle, exercise, nutrition, meditation, quality of sleep, and so on.

Self-Investigation: Level of self-awareness this week—discovery, examination, and personal development through reading and writing, expansion of personal knowledge, self-communication, and so on.

Creativity/Entertainment: Level of adventure, enjoyment of hobbies, art, laughter, amusement, and so on this week.

Relationships: Level of communication this week—with family, friends, my community, and so on.

Work/Education: Level of investment in work, career, homemaking (management of the household), and education this week.

Goal Setter	My goal(s) for next week are... Describe EATs.	What step(s) will I take next week to achieve my goal(s)?
Gratitude and Forgiveness		
Health		
Self-Investigation		
Creativity/ Entertainment		
Relationships		
Work/ Education		

Life is a melody, and you are the composer.

Date_____**Time**_____

Tip: With your eyes closed, take a few slow, deep inhalations and exhalations. Review your day, open your eyes, and begin.

1. **Today**, after reviewing my day, what **E**motions, **A**ctions/behaviors, and **T**houghts (**EAT**s) arise?

2. **Today**, what made (and still makes) me happy? Describe **EAT**s.

3. **Today**, how did I love myself? Describe **EAT**s.

4. **Today**, how did I love others? Describe **EAT**s.

5. **Today**, what did I learn about myself? What did I learn in general? Describe the **EAT**s created from the lessons.

6. **Today**, did I accomplish the goal(s) I set for myself yesterday? (Yes/No) If not, what steps will I take to accomplish them?
What is/are my goal(s) for tomorrow?
By accomplishing my goal(s), what will it/they allow me to achieve?
How will my goal(s) influence my **EAT**s?

7. **Today**, for whom and for what am I grateful? Describe the reasons. Describe **EAT**s.

Great things are done by a series of
small things brought together.
—Vincent Van Gogh

Date_____**Time**_____

Tip: With your eyes closed, take a few slow, deep inhalations and exhalations.
Review your day, open your eyes, and begin.

1. **Today**, after reviewing my day, what **E**motions, **A**ctions/behaviors, and **T**houghts (**EAT**s) arise?

2. **Today**, what made (and still makes) me happy? Describe **EAT**s.

3. **Today**, how did I love myself? Describe **EAT**s.

4. **Today**, how did I love others? Describe **EAT**s.

5. **Today**, what did I learn about myself? What did I learn in general? Describe the **EAT**s created from the lessons.

6. **Today**, did I accomplish the goal(s) I set for myself yesterday? (Yes/No) If not, what steps will I take to accomplish them?
    What is/are my goal(s) for tomorrow?
    By accomplishing my goal(s), what will it/they allow me to achieve? How will my goal(s) influence my **EAT**s?

7. **Today**, for whom and for what am I grateful? Describe the reasons. Describe **EAT**s.

Life is a succession of lessons which
must be lived to be understood.
—HELEN KELLER

Date_____**Time**_____

Tip: With your eyes closed, take a few slow, deep inhalations and exhalations. Review your day, open your eyes, and begin.

1. **Today**, after reviewing my day, what **E**motions, **A**ctions/behaviors, and **T**houghts (**EAT**s) arise?

2. **Today**, what made (and still makes) me happy? Describe **EAT**s.

3. **Today**, how did I love myself? Describe **EAT**s.

4. **Today**, how did I love others? Describe **EAT**s.

5. **Today**, what did I learn about myself? What did I learn in general? Describe the **EAT**s created from the lessons.

6. **Today**, did I accomplish the goal(s) I set for myself yesterday? (Yes/No) If not, what steps will I take to accomplish them?
   What is/are my goal(s) for tomorrow?
   By accomplishing my goal(s), what will it/they allow me to achieve?
   How will my goal(s) influence my **EAT**s?

7. **Today**, for whom and for what am I grateful? Describe the reasons. Describe **EAT**s.

The secret of getting ahead is getting started.
—Mark Twain

Me

Date_____**Time**_____

Tip: With your eyes closed, take a few slow, deep inhalations and exhalations.
Review your day, open your eyes, and begin.

1. **Today**, after reviewing my day, what **E**motions, **A**ctions/behaviors, and **T**houghts (**EAT**s) arise?

2. **Today**, what made (and still makes) me happy? Describe **EAT**s.

3. **Today**, how did I love myself? Describe **EAT**s.

4. **Today**, how did I love others? Describe **EAT**s.

5. **Today**, what did I learn about myself? What did I learn in general? Describe the **EAT**s created from the lessons.

6. **Today**, did I accomplish the goal(s) I set for myself yesterday? (Yes/No) If not, what steps will I take to accomplish them?
What is/are my goal(s) for tomorrow?
By accomplishing my goal(s), what will it/they allow me to achieve?
How will my goal(s) influence my **EAT**s?

7. **Today**, for whom and for what am I grateful? Describe the reasons. Describe **EAT**s.

The only person you are destined to become
is the person you decide to be.
—RALPH WALDO EMERSON

Date_____Time_____

Tip: With your eyes closed, take a few slow, deep inhalations and exhalations.
Review your day, open your eyes, and begin.

1. **Today**, after reviewing my day, what **E**motions, **A**ctions/behaviors, and **T**houghts (**EAT**s) arise?

2. **Today**, what made (and still makes) me happy? Describe **EAT**s.

3. **Today**, how did I love myself? Describe **EAT**s.

4. **Today**, how did I love others? Describe **EAT**s.

5. **Today**, what did I learn about myself? What did I learn in general? Describe the **EAT**s created from the lessons.

6. **Today**, did I accomplish the goal(s) I set for myself yesterday? (Yes/No) If not, what steps will I take to accomplish them?
   What is/are my goal(s) for tomorrow?
   By accomplishing my goal(s), what will it/they allow me to achieve?
   How will my goal(s) influence my **EAT**s?

7. **Today**, for whom and for what am I grateful? Describe the reasons. Describe **EAT**s.

Take a chance - it's the best way to test
yourself, have fun and push boundaries.
—RICHARD BRANSON

Date_____Time_____

Tip: With your eyes closed, take a few slow, deep inhalations and exhalations.
Review your day, open your eyes, and begin.

1. **Today**, after reviewing my day, what **E**motions, **A**ctions/behaviors, and **T**houghts (**EAT**s) arise?

2. **Today**, what made (and still makes) me happy? Describe **EAT**s.

3. **Today**, how did I love myself? Describe **EAT**s.

4. **Today**, how did I love others? Describe **EAT**s.

5. **Today**, what did I learn about myself? What did I learn in general? Describe the **EAT**s created from the lessons.

6. **Today**, did I accomplish the goal(s) I set for myself yesterday? (Yes/No) If not, what steps will I take to accomplish them?
What is/are my goal(s) for tomorrow?
By accomplishing my goal(s), what will it/they allow me to achieve?
How will my goal(s) influence my **EAT**s?

7. **Today**, for whom and for what am I grateful? Describe the reasons. Describe **EAT**s.

Be happy for this moment. This moment is your life.
—OMAR KHAYYAM

Date_____**Time**_____

Tip: With your eyes closed, take a few slow, deep inhalations and exhalations. Review your day, open your eyes, and begin.

1. **Today**, after reviewing my day, what **E**motions, **A**ctions/behaviors, and **T**houghts (**EAT**s) arise?

2. **Today**, what made (and still makes) me happy? Describe **EAT**s.

3. **Today**, how did I love myself? Describe **EAT**s.

4. **Today**, how did I love others? Describe **EAT**s.

5. **Today**, what did I learn about myself? What did I learn in general? Describe the **EAT**s created from the lessons.

6. **Today**, did I accomplish the goal(s) I set for myself yesterday? (Yes/No) If not, what steps will I take to accomplish them?
What is/are my goal(s) for tomorrow?
By accomplishing my goal(s), what will it/they allow me to achieve?
How will my goal(s) influence my **EAT**s?

7. **Today**, for whom and for what am I grateful? Describe the reasons. Describe **EAT**s.

Always turn a negative situation into a positive situation.
—MICHAEL JORDAN

This Week's Melody

To further your self-discovery and self-awareness this week place music notes (♩) or dots on the music lines below. Each music note/dot will represent the tone/sound you chose to create in the following subjects this week:

♩The top position of the music note/dot on the music lines below represents a high level of fulfillment.

♩The middle position of the music note/dot on the music lines below represents a partial level of fulfillment.

♩The bottom position of the music note/dot on the music lines below represents a desire for further fulfillment.

Gratitude and Forgiveness: Level of thankfulness and forgiveness this week—gratitude and forgiveness for myself and others, using the events that happened *for* me this week.

Health: Level of body nourishment this week—healthy lifestyle, exercise, nutrition, meditation, quality of sleep, and so on.

Self-Investigation: Level of self-awareness this week—discovery, examination, and personal development through reading and writing, expansion of personal knowledge, self-communication, and so on.

Creativity/Entertainment: Level of adventure, enjoyment of hobbies, art, laughter, amusement, and so on this week.

Relationships: Level of communication this week—with family, friends, my community, and so on.

Work/Education: Level of investment in work, career, homemaking (management of the household), and education this week.

Goal Setter	My goal(s) for next week are... Describe EATs.	What step(s) will I take next week to achieve my goal(s)?
Gratitude and Forgiveness		
Health		
Self-Investigation		
Creativity/ Entertainment		
Relationships		
Work/ Education		

Life is a melody, and you are the composer.

Date_____**Time**_____

Tip: With your eyes closed, take a few slow, deep inhalations and exhalations.
Review your day, open your eyes, and begin.

1. **Today**, after reviewing my day, what **E**motions, **A**ctions/behaviors, and **T**houghts (**EAT**s) arise?

2. **Today**, what made (and still makes) me happy? Describe **EAT**s.

3. **Today**, how did I love myself? Describe **EAT**s.

4. **Today**, how did I love others? Describe **EAT**s.

5. **Today**, what did I learn about myself? What did I learn in general? Describe the **EAT**s created from the lessons.

6. **Today**, did I accomplish the goal(s) I set for myself yesterday? (Yes/No) If not, what steps will I take to accomplish them?
   What is/are my goal(s) for tomorrow?
   By accomplishing my goal(s), what will it/they allow me to achieve?
   How will my goal(s) influence my **EAT**s?

7. **Today**, for whom and for what am I grateful? Describe the reasons. Describe **EAT**s.

Where there is love there is life.
—Mahatma Gandhi

Date_____**Time**_____

Tip: With your eyes closed, take a few slow, deep inhalations and exhalations.
Review your day, open your eyes, and begin.

1. **Today**, after reviewing my day, what **E**motions, **A**ctions/behaviors, and **T**houghts (**EAT**s) arise?

2. **Today**, what made (and still makes) me happy? Describe **EAT**s.

3. **Today**, how did I love myself? Describe **EAT**s.

4. **Today**, how did I love others? Describe **EAT**s.

5. **Today**, what did I learn about myself? What did I learn in general? Describe the **EAT**s created from the lessons.

6. **Today**, did I accomplish the goal(s) I set for myself yesterday? (Yes/No) If not, what steps will I take to accomplish them?
What is/are my goal(s) for tomorrow?
By accomplishing my goal(s), what will it/they allow me to achieve?
How will my goal(s) influence my **EAT**s?

7. **Today**, for whom and for what am I grateful? Describe the reasons. Describe **EAT**s.

Never, ever, never give up.
—WINSTON CHURCHILL

Date_____**Time**_____

Tip: With your eyes closed, take a few slow, deep inhalations and exhalations.
Review your day, open your eyes, and begin.

1. **Today**, after reviewing my day, what **E**motions, **A**ctions/behaviors, and **T**houghts (**EAT**s) arise?

2. **Today**, what made (and still makes) me happy? Describe **EAT**s.

3. **Today**, how did I love myself? Describe **EAT**s.

4. **Today**, how did I love others? Describe **EAT**s.

5. **Today**, what did I learn about myself? What did I learn in general? Describe the **EAT**s created from the lessons.

6. **Today**, did I accomplish the goal(s) I set for myself yesterday? (Yes/No) If not, what steps will I take to accomplish them?
What is/are my goal(s) for tomorrow?
By accomplishing my goal(s), what will it/they allow me to achieve?
How will my goal(s) influence my **EAT**s?

7. **Today**, for whom and for what am I grateful? Describe the reasons. Describe **EAT**s.

Don't wait. The time will never be just right.
—NAPOLEON HILL

Date_____**Time**_____

Tip: With your eyes closed, take a few slow, deep inhalations and exhalations. Review your day, open your eyes, and begin.

1. **Today**, after reviewing my day, what **E**motions, **A**ctions/behaviors, and **T**houghts (**EAT**s) arise?

2. **Today**, what made (and still makes) me happy? Describe **EAT**s.

3. **Today**, how did I love myself? Describe **EAT**s.

4. **Today**, how did I love others? Describe **EAT**s.

5. **Today**, what did I learn about myself? What did I learn in general? Describe the **EAT**s created from the lessons.

6. **Today**, did I accomplish the goal(s) I set for myself yesterday? (Yes/No) If not, what steps will I take to accomplish them?
   What is/are my goal(s) for tomorrow?
   By accomplishing my goal(s), what will it/they allow me to achieve?
   How will my goal(s) influence my **EAT**s?

7. **Today**, for whom and for what am I grateful? Describe the reasons. Describe **EAT**s.

When a person really desires something, all the universe
conspires to help that person to realize his dream.
—PAULO COELHO

Date_____**Time**_____

Tip: With your eyes closed, take a few slow, deep inhalations and exhalations.
Review your day, open your eyes, and begin.

1. **Today**, after reviewing my day, what **E**motions, **A**ctions/behaviors, and **T**houghts (**EAT**s) arise?

2. **Today**, what made (and still makes) me happy? Describe **EAT**s.

3. **Today**, how did I love myself? Describe **EAT**s.

4. **Today**, how did I love others? Describe **EAT**s.

5. **Today**, what did I learn about myself? What did I learn in general? Describe the **EAT**s created from the lessons.

6. **Today**, did I accomplish the goal(s) I set for myself yesterday? (Yes/No) If not, what steps will I take to accomplish them?
What is/are my goal(s) for tomorrow?
By accomplishing my goal(s), what will it/they allow me to achieve? How will my goal(s) influence my **EAT**s?

7. **Today**, for whom and for what am I grateful? Describe the reasons. Describe **EAT**s.

If you think you're too small to have an impact,
try going to bed with a mosquito in the room.
—ANITA RODDICK

Date_____**Time**_____

Tip: With your eyes closed, take a few slow, deep inhalations and exhalations. Review your day, open your eyes, and begin.

1. **Today**, after reviewing my day, what **E**motions, **A**ctions/behaviors, and **T**houghts (**EAT**s) arise?

2. **Today**, what made (and still makes) me happy? Describe **EAT**s.

3. **Today**, how did I love myself? Describe **EAT**s.

4. **Today**, how did I love others? Describe **EAT**s.

5. **Today**, what did I learn about myself? What did I learn in general? Describe the **EAT**s created from the lessons.

6. **Today**, did I accomplish the goal(s) I set for myself yesterday? (Yes/No) If not, what steps will I take to accomplish them?
   What is/are my goal(s) for tomorrow?
   By accomplishing my goal(s), what will it/they allow me to achieve? How will my goal(s) influence my **EAT**s?

7. **Today**, for whom and for what am I grateful? Describe the reasons. Describe **EAT**s.

There are no secrets to success. This is the result of preparation, hard work and learning from mistakes.
—Colin Powell

Date_____**Time**_____

Tip: With your eyes closed, take a few slow, deep inhalations and exhalations. Review your day, open your eyes, and begin.

1. **Today**, after reviewing my day, what **E**motions, **A**ctions/behaviors, and **T**houghts (**EAT**s) arise?

2. **Today**, what made (and still makes) me happy? Describe **EAT**s.

3. **Today**, how did I love myself? Describe **EAT**s.

4. **Today**, how did I love others? Describe **EAT**s.

5. **Today**, what did I learn about myself? What did I learn in general? Describe the **EAT**s created from the lessons.

6. **Today**, did I accomplish the goal(s) I set for myself yesterday? (Yes/No) If not, what steps will I take to accomplish them?
   What is/are my goal(s) for tomorrow?
   By accomplishing my goal(s), what will it/they allow me to achieve?
   How will my goal(s) influence my **EAT**s?

7. **Today**, for whom and for what am I grateful? Describe the reasons. Describe **EAT**s.

Either write something worth reading or
do something worth writing about.
—Benjamin Franklin

This Week's Melody

To further your self-discovery and self-awareness this week place music notes (♩) or dots on the music lines below. Each music note/dot will represent the tone/sound you chose to create in the following subjects this week:

♪The top position of the music note/dot on the music lines below represents a high level of fulfillment.

♪The middle position of the music note/dot on the music lines below represents a partial level of fulfillment.

♪The bottom position of the music note/dot on the music lines below represents a desire for further fulfillment.

Gratitude and Forgiveness: Level of thankfulness and forgiveness this week—gratitude and forgiveness for myself and others, using the events that happened *for* me this week.

Health: Level of body nourishment this week—healthy lifestyle, exercise, nutrition, meditation, quality of sleep, and so on.

Self-Investigation: Level of self-awareness this week—discovery, examination, and personal development through reading and writing, expansion of personal knowledge, self-communication, and so on.

Creativity/Entertainment: Level of adventure, enjoyment of hobbies, art, laughter, amusement, and so on this week.

Relationships: Level of communication this week—with family, friends, my community, and so on.

Work/Education: Level of investment in work, career, homemaking (management of the household), and education this week.

Goal Setter	My goal(s) for next week are... Describe EATs.	What step(s) will I take next week to achieve my goal(s)?
Gratitude and Forgiveness		
Health		
Self-Investigation		
Creativity/ Entertainment		
Relationships		
Work/ Education		

Life is a melody, and you are the composer.

Date_____**Time**_____

Tip: With your eyes closed, take a few slow, deep inhalations and exhalations.
Review your day, open your eyes, and begin.

1. **Today**, after reviewing my day, what **E**motions, **A**ctions/behaviors, and **T**houghts (**EAT**s) arise?

2. **Today**, what made (and still makes) me happy? Describe **EAT**s.

3. **Today**, how did I love myself? Describe **EAT**s.

4. **Today**, how did I love others? Describe **EAT**s.

5. **Today**, what did I learn about myself? What did I learn in general? Describe the **EAT**s created from the lessons.

6. **Today**, did I accomplish the goal(s) I set for myself yesterday? (Yes/No) If not, what steps will I take to accomplish them? What is/are my goal(s) for tomorrow? By accomplishing my goal(s), what will it/they allow me to achieve? How will my goal(s) influence my **EAT**s?

7. **Today**, for whom and for what am I grateful? Describe the reasons. Describe **EAT**s.

Those who are not brave enough to take risks will not achieve anything in life.
—Muhammad Ali

Date_____**Time**_____

Tip: With your eyes closed, take a few slow, deep inhalations and exhalations.
Review your day, open your eyes, and begin.

1. **Today**, after reviewing my day, what **E**motions, **A**ctions/behav-
iors, and **T**houghts (**EAT**s) arise?

2. **Today**, what made (and still makes) me happy? Describe **EAT**s.

3. **Today**, how did I love myself? Describe **EAT**s.

4. **Today**, how did I love others? Describe **EAT**s.

5. **Today**, what did I learn about myself? What did I learn in general? Describe the **EAT**s created from the lessons.

6. **Today**, did I accomplish the goal(s) I set for myself yesterday? (Yes/No) If not, what steps will I take to accomplish them?
What is/are my goal(s) for tomorrow?
By accomplishing my goal(s), what will it/they allow me to achieve?
How will my goal(s) influence my **EAT**s?

7. **Today**, for whom and for what am I grateful? Describe the reasons. Describe **EAT**s.

Everything has beauty, but not everyone sees it.
—CONFUCIUS

Date_____**Time**_____

Tip: With your eyes closed, take a few slow, deep inhalations and exhalations. Review your day, open your eyes, and begin.

1. **Today**, after reviewing my day, what **E**motions, **A**ctions/behaviors, and **T**houghts (**EAT**s) arise?

2. **Today**, what made (and still makes) me happy? Describe **EAT**s.

3. **Today**, how did I love myself? Describe **EAT**s.

4. **Today**, how did I love others? Describe **EAT**s.

5. **Today**, what did I learn about myself? What did I learn in general? Describe the **EAT**s created from the lessons.

6. **Today**, did I accomplish the goal(s) I set for myself yesterday? (Yes/No) If not, what steps will I take to accomplish them? What is/are my goal(s) for tomorrow? By accomplishing my goal(s), what will it/they allow me to achieve? How will my goal(s) influence my **EAT**s?

7. **Today**, for whom and for what am I grateful? Describe the reasons. Describe **EAT**s.

> Happiness lies in the joy of achievement
> and the thrill of creative effort.
> —Franklin D. Roosevelt

Date_____Time_____

Tip: With your eyes closed, take a few slow, deep inhalations and exhalations.
Review your day, open your eyes, and begin.

1. **Today**, after reviewing my day, what **E**motions, **A**ctions/behaviors, and **T**houghts (**EAT**s) arise?

2. **Today**, what made (and still makes) me happy? Describe **EAT**s.

3. **Today**, how did I love myself? Describe **EAT**s.

4. **Today**, how did I love others? Describe **EAT**s.

5. **Today**, what did I learn about myself? What did I learn in general? Describe the **EAT**s created from the lessons.

6. **Today**, did I accomplish the goal(s) I set for myself yesterday? (Yes/No) If not, what steps will I take to accomplish them?
What is/are my goal(s) for tomorrow?
By accomplishing my goal(s), what will it/they allow me to achieve?
How will my goal(s) influence my **EAT**s?

7. **Today**, for whom and for what am I grateful? Describe the reasons. Describe **EAT**s.

Your attitude, not your aptitude, will
determine your altitude.
—ZIG ZIGLAR

Me

Date_____**Time**_____

Tip: With your eyes closed, take a few slow, deep inhalations and exhalations.
Review your day, open your eyes, and begin.

1. **Today**, after reviewing my day, what **E**motions, **A**ctions/behaviors, and **T**houghts (**EAT**s) arise?

2. **Today**, what made (and still makes) me happy? Describe **EAT**s.

3. **Today**, how did I love myself? Describe **EAT**s.

4. **Today**, how did I love others? Describe **EAT**s.

5. **Today**, what did I learn about myself? What did I learn in general? Describe the **EAT**s created from the lessons.

6. **Today**, did I accomplish the goal(s) I set for myself yesterday? (Yes/No) If not, what steps will I take to accomplish them?
    What is/are my goal(s) for tomorrow?
    By accomplishing my goal(s), what will it/they allow me to achieve? How will my goal(s) influence my **EAT**s?

7. **Today**, for whom and for what am I grateful? Describe the reasons. Describe **EAT**s.

When the mind is pure, joy follows like
a shadow that never leaves.
—BUDDHA

Date_____**Time**_____

Tip: With your eyes closed, take a few slow, deep inhalations and exhalations.
Review your day, open your eyes, and begin.

1. **Today**, after reviewing my day, what **E**motions, **A**ctions/behaviors, and **T**houghts (**EAT**s) arise?

2. **Today**, what made (and still makes) me happy? Describe **EAT**s.

3. **Today**, how did I love myself? Describe **EAT**s.

4. **Today**, how did I love others? Describe **EAT**s.

5. **Today**, what did I learn about myself? What did I learn in general? Describe the **EAT**s created from the lessons.

6. **Today**, did I accomplish the goal(s) I set for myself yesterday? (Yes/No) If not, what steps will I take to accomplish them?
   What is/are my goal(s) for tomorrow?
   By accomplishing my goal(s), what will it/they allow me to achieve?
   How will my goal(s) influence my **EAT**s?

7. **Today**, for whom and for what am I grateful? Describe the reasons. Describe **EAT**s.

Inspiration exists, but it must find us working.
—PABLO PICASSO

Date_____**Time**_____

Tip: With your eyes closed, take a few slow, deep inhalations and exhalations.
Review your day, open your eyes, and begin.

1. **Today**, after reviewing my day, what **E**motions, **A**ctions/behaviors, and **T**houghts (**EAT**s) arise?

2. **Today**, what made (and still makes) me happy? Describe **EAT**s.

3. **Today**, how did I love myself? Describe **EAT**s.

4. **Today**, how did I love others? Describe **EAT**s.

5. **Today**, what did I learn about myself? What did I learn in general? Describe the **EAT**s created from the lessons.

6. **Today**, did I accomplish the goal(s) I set for myself yesterday? (Yes/No) If not, what steps will I take to accomplish them?
   What is/are my goal(s) for tomorrow?
   By accomplishing my goal(s), what will it/they allow me to achieve?
   How will my goal(s) influence my **EAT**s?

7. **Today**, for whom and for what am I grateful? Describe the reasons. Describe **EAT**s.

Motivation is what gets you going.
Habit is what keeps you going.
—JOHN ROHN

This Week's Melody

To further your self-discovery and self-awareness this week place music notes (♩) or dots on the music lines below. Each music note/dot will represent the tone/sound you chose to create in the following subjects this week:

♪The top position of the music note/dot on the music lines below represents a high level of fulfillment.

♪The middle position of the music note/dot on the music lines below represents a partial level of fulfillment.

♩The bottom position of the music note/dot on the music lines below represents a desire for further fulfillment.

Gratitude and Forgiveness: Level of thankfulness and forgiveness this week—gratitude and forgiveness for myself and others, using the events that happened *for* me this week.

Health: Level of body nourishment this week—healthy lifestyle, exercise, nutrition, meditation, quality of sleep, and so on.

Self-Investigation: Level of self-awareness this week—discovery, examination, and personal development through reading and writing, expansion of personal knowledge, self-communication, and so on.

Creativity/Entertainment: Level of adventure, enjoyment of hobbies, art, laughter, amusement, and so on this week.

Relationships: Level of communication this week—with family, friends, my community, and so on.

Work/Education: Level of investment in work, career, homemaking (management of the household), and education this week.

Goal Setter	My goal(s) for next week are... Describe EATs.	What step(s) will I take next week to achieve my goal(s)?
Gratitude and Forgiveness		
Health		
Self-Investigation		
Creativity/ Entertainment		
Relationships		
Work/ Education		

Life is a melody, and you are the composer.

Congratulations for choosing to self-communicate and become more consciously aware of yourself and your surroundings!

Be proud of who you are!
You are worth it!

We would love to communicate with you and discover how your **11 week~Guided Journey by Journal** affected your life. To keep in touch and for additional information, blogs, life exercises, and more to further your communication skills, self-awareness and personal development, please visit www.hometopurpose.com.

No one knows you better than you know yourself!

THANK YOU! ☺

About the Author

JENNIFER AYERS-BELINKIS IS a philanthropist, NLP Master Practitioner, Aromatherapist, Bach Flower Practitioner, and with her first publication— *Me: Life Guide and Guided Journey by Journal*—an author. She is a nature lover at heart, a life investigator, and a DIY upcycler who is fascinated with the **Environment~Body~Soul:Minds~Spirit** connection. She proclaims to be head over heels in love with life, herself, her husband, their four children, and their frisky dog.

Jennifer was born and raised in Virginia and at the age of twenty-four moved to Israel where she resides today. She holds American and Israeli dual citizenship and retains a deep love for both countries.

To further her passion of purpose, Ayers-Belinkis established **H**ome t**O** **P**urpos**E** (**HOPE**), a nonprofit organization that inspires and encourages each individual to discover who they truly are and to pursue their passions in life. A part of the proceeds from *Me: Life Guide and Guided Journey by Journal* will go to support **HOPE** and its mission.

You are welcome to experience **HOPE** at www.hometopurpose.com.

Made in the USA
Lexington, KY
15 November 2019